THE GREAT
PASTA
COOKBOOK

Introduced by Rosemary Moon
Photography by Peter Barry
Illustrations by Madeleine David
Designed by Claire Leighton and Richard Hawke
Edited by Jillian Stewart

CLB 3225
© 1993 Colour Library Books Ltd., Godalming, Surrey.
All rights reserved.
Printed and bound by Tien Wah Press (PTE) Ltd, Singapore
ISBN 1 85833 043 2

THE GREAT
PASTA
COOKBOOK

JUDITH FERGUSON

Colour Library Books

Contents

Introduction

The History of Pasta

The proven origins of pasta, like those of tea, coffee, cheese and other staples of our modern international diet, are lost in time. Now, if you are Chinese or Italian and read this you will doubtless be enraged, for both nations have been claiming the invention of pasta for centuries – but I am prudently going to keep out of the argument!

Suffice it to say that as cereal crops have been farmed for over 8,000 years, and as pasta is simply a paste, usually of wheat flour with eggs or water, it is reasonable to assume that it has been made, cut and used dried or fresh for many hundreds of years.

Following Marco Polo's visit to China in 1270 there were detailed reports of the eating of noodles, hence the idea that he may have brought pasta back from his travels. However, vermicelli – the thread pasta most akin to Chinese noodles – was a staple part of the Italian diet long before the thirteenth century. Indeed, the Etruscans may have developed pasta from an ancient Greek recipe for a dough cake, cut into strips and called "laganon" – the word from which lasagne is surely derived. There is also a theory that it has Arabic origins – the word "itriyah", meaning string or little threads as a description of spaghetti, could have led to the word "tri", an early term for pasta. There is a Spaghetti Museum at Pontedassio on the Italian Riviera, but I fear the exhibits may be biased in favour of the Italian claims to have invented pasta.

However pasta first came to be made, three cheers that it was, for it is certainly one of the most versatile of foods and is now a great favourite with people all round the world.

Pasta Comes in All Shapes and Sizes

Identifying pasta shapes is quite an art. There are many different tubes, twirls and flat bits of varying widths – and to confuse matters further most regions of Italy have different names for each shape! The best known example of this is that tagliatelle, the ribbon pasta that is a speciality of the Italian Bologna region, is known as fettucini in Rome. To further confuse the issue *macaroni* is actually a generic name for all types of dried pasta, although it is more often used to describe large, hollow

Left: there are numerous commercial pasta shapes – spirals, tagliatelle, and spaghetti are among the most popular and are available in a variety of thicknesses and colours.

Above: pasta shapes such as pasta bows, shells, and penne are mainly served with a textured sauce containing meat, fish or vegetables, for example ham, prawn or aubergine.

spaghetti, either in long strips or short cut.

There is no real purpose in having a choice of almost 600 different pastas – the result of rivalry between the largest of the Italian manufacturers, each of whom set out to have the most comprehensive catalogue of specialist pasta shapes. It is the gastronomic equivalent of the state-of-the-art washing machine with twenty wash programmes, when only two get regular use!

Home-made and Dried Pastas

There are two main groups of pastas – *pasta secca*, the commercially prepared dried pasta, usually made from a flour and water paste; and *pasta all'uovo* or *pasta fatta in casa*, home-made egg pasta. Home-made pasta relies on the skill of the maker with a rolling pin and sharp knife, or a simple pasta machine which passes the dough between rollers to create a limited selection of shapes. A much greater variety of pastas is available dried, where the dough can be extruded commercially to form tubes, twirls and countless other shapes.

Pasta can be classified into five main groups:
Shapes for coating with a smooth sauce This includes spaghetti, tagliatelle, fusilli and cappelletti. These are all fine strands or small shapes which readily absorb a smooth-textured sauce. The pasta should be tossed in the sauce before serving to make a complete dish – it is a very foreign idea to serve Spaghetti Bolognese as a bed of spaghetti topped with a mound of meat sauce with a smattering of Parmesan cheese on the very top.

Shapes that catch the good bits! I include many of the larger pastas in this category – farfalle, large fusilli and penne, rigatoni shells and large macaroni – and usually prepare a textured sauce to serve with the pasta, with pieces of ham, salami, prawn, mushroom or other vegetable dice. Tossing the pasta in the sauce before serving will create pockets of good things in amongst the pasta to surprise your tastebuds!

Pastas for stuffing Commercially stuffed pastas are available, mainly ravioli or tortellini, and these require boiling before being served in a sauce or melted, flavoured butter. Ravioli can be prepared at home, widening the choice of stuffings for the dish, and is made from strips of lasagne. Cannelloni should be boiled, stuffed and then baked, whereas the large shells, conchiglie rigate, are boiled before stuffing to be served hot or cold as a starter.

Above: one of the most familiar pastas – lasagne – is used for baking, the numerous shapes of tiny pastina for soups and desserts, and large tubes such as cannelloni for stuffing.

Ravioli, cappelletti and tortellini – sealed, stuffed pasta shapes – are available ready stuffed, dried or fresh, or you can make your own.

Lasagne and other pastas for baking These, after initial boiling, become an integral part of baked dishes such as lasagne *al forno*, lasagne from the oven, or baked pasta. The Maltese use large macaroni tubes for a wonderful pie, sandwiching the pasta between layers of meat sauce under a pastry crust.

Fine pastas for soups Vermicelli and other strands of pasta are most commonly used for soups, but novelty shapes, be they alphabet letters, flowers or miniature spacemen, all known by the general term *pastina*, have special appeal for children everywhere, and may also be used to thicken stews and casseroles.

Coloured and Flavoured Pastas

The pale yellow colour of pasta is derived from the eggs and flour used in the dough. Most commercial pastas are made from durum, a hard wheat with a slightly grainy texture when milled. Home-made pasta dough is best made with strong bread flour, also milled from a hard wheat.

Wholemeal pasta was pioneered in the UK and actually shipped to Italy! It is made from durum wheat which is carefully milled to retain some of the husk. The pasta was developed to satisfy the growing interest in wholefoods and healthfoods and became popular at the same time as brown rice. I find it almost impossible to make wholemeal pasta at home as it is very difficult to get the dough at the right consistency with the coarser grain of the flour. Wholemeal pasta, like wholemeal pastry, has a slightly harder, drier texture than its regular equivalent.

Pasta Verde simply means green pasta, the colour of which is usually obtained from spinach in a very fine puree, or from spinach juice. The most common green pastas are lasagne and tagliatelle. A lovely flecked green pasta can be made at home by adding very finely chopped herbs to the dough.

Black Pasta is the choice of the design-conscious cook! It will have to be home-made and is coloured with the ink from squid or cuttlefish and is therefore most suitable for serving with a fish sauce. It is important not to make the dough too wet whilst striving to attain a strong black colour.

Other Vegetable Pastas include carrot (orange), beetroot (dark red) and saffron (bright yellow). The colours are obtained by adding juices extracted from the vegetables

flavour between commercially coloured pastas – textures are slightly different but the actual flavour only changes, for me, when I make the dough at home. Dried pasta made in Italy tends to expand slightly more during cooking than that made elsewhere, in the same way as home-made pasta does, giving a softer dish when the accompanying sauce is added. The Italian manufacturers in Naples claim their pastas to be the best owing to the quality of their water supply – whether this is true or not is for you to decide, but it does illustrate how fiercely proud the Italians are of their pasta-making art.

Left: add finely chopped spinach to your pasta dough to make pasta verdi. Below: knead the dough thoroughly to ensure that the spinach is evenly distributed.

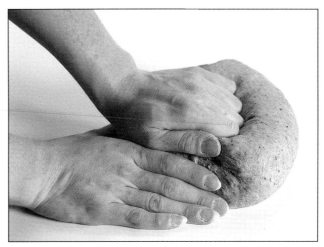

and they do look effective – although I think they look better in the storage jar than on a plate as the colourings tend to wash out during cooking. (Saffron strands are added to the flour and kneaded through the dough to spread the colour.) Tomato pasta is often sold with white and green pastas to give a three coloured selection, especially good for pasta salads.

I cannot honestly say that I notice any difference in

Below: pasta flavoured and coloured with herbs, spinach, squid-ink, saffron and beetroot. Other common flavourings and colourings include tomato, carrot and turmeric.

Buying Pasta

A good variety of shapes is available in just about every supermarket and grocery shop, and most now keep packets of fresh pasta as well as the familiar dried varieties.

A few packets of dried pasta in the storecupboard provides the basis for a wide variety of quick, nutritious and satisfying meals. Thanks to its popularity pasta has a quick turnover so it is reasonable to expect a shelf life of around twelve months or more on each packet that you buy. Store in the manufacturers' packaging until required. If the whole packet is not used at once, reseal the bag with a wire tie or clip, or better still, store in an air-tight container.

Commercially prepared, pre-packed pasta usually has a life of 7-10 days when it leaves the factory. It should be stored in the 'fridge or chiller and cooks more quickly than dried pasta (fresh pasta is cooked when it floats to the top of the pan). Towards the end of its life this type of pasta becomes dry and almost crusty, but is good when eaten fresh.

I think it is true to say that the Italians would have no knowledge of commercially prepared fresh pasta, sold in packets. Many delicatessens and grocery shops sell their own pasta, freshly made each day, as do countless Italian shops throughout the world. I find that this and homemade dough are the only alternatives worth considering to a good quality dried pasta.

Making your Own Pasta

This is great fun! It requires time for the preparation and a little practise to get the dough just right, but the flavour of the home-made dough makes it well worth persevering. Many people say that if you can make a good pastry you can make a good pasta – as my pastry making is not brilliant, I liken the preparation of pasta dough more to that of bread dough, as both require kneading. The use of a pasta machine does make the preparation of the shaped pasta much quicker – the purist would scoff at such culinary aids, but I think my pasta machine is one of the best pieces of equipment in my kitchen.

The basic dough could not be more simple:
   450g/1lb plain white flour
    (preferably strong bread flour)
    4 eggs, lightly beaten
    water or olive oil
This will make sufficient pasta for 6 people.

Below: making pasta yourself is great fun and not difficult. Make a well in the centre of the flour and add the lightly-beaten eggs. Gradually mix the eggs into the flour to form a fairly dry dough. A little olive oil or water can be added at this stage if necessary.

Mixing the Dough

The pasta masters all say you should place the flour in a mound on the worktop (or, better still, a large marble surface), add the eggs and combine into a dough with your fingers, gradually mixing the flour into the liquid to form the paste. The success of this relies heavily on the dexterity of your fingers and your ability not to hurry – one false move, jabbing your fingers violently through the wall of flour, and there is egg all down the fronts of your kitchen units. Call me a coward, but I mix my dough in a bowl. The important thing is at least to finish the mixing by hand, to allow you to feel the texture of the dough, which should be fairly dry. I add a little olive oil or water at this stage of the mixing if the dough requires extra moisture, but the eggs are often sufficient by themselves (UK size 2 or 3).

As for bread making, do not attempt to incorporate into the dough any dry pieces of mix in the bottom of the bowl or on the edges of the working area – these will form hard lumps in the finished pasta. Form the dough into a ball on a lightly floured work surface and knead until it is smooth and elastic – this will take 5-10 minutes, depending on your mood and how rhythmic your kneading is. Push the dough away from you with the heel of your hand and then fold it back towards you – it is easier to do than to write about!

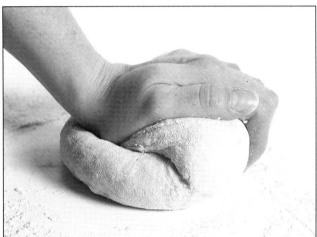

Left and below: form the dough into a ball and knead it until it is smooth and elastic. If rolling out by hand, it is the right thickness when you can see your work top through it. Leave the dough to rest by draping it over the back of a chair.

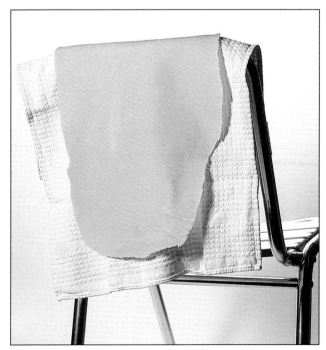

Resting

Some chefs suggest leaving the dough to rest at this point, covered with a bowl to prevent it from drying out. However, I prefer to leave it after the initial shaping and before the dough is cut into the final shape required. (I'm not sure whether this is because I feel I'm closer to eating if I press on at this stage!) Resting now is more critical if you are to roll the dough by hand – if it keeps "springing back" when you try to roll it, it needs a rest – so cover with a bowl and leave for 20-30 minutes before trying to roll it out again.

Rolling

If you do not have a pasta machine you will need a very long rolling pin, about 50-55cm or 24 inches in length, in order to roll the dough smoothly and evenly. A wooden broom handle is a good alternative. I often suggest using a milk or wine bottle if there is no rolling pin to hand for pastry, but you really do need the length for pasta so a bottle is not a suitable alternative.

Divide the dough into two and roll each half into a large circle, turning the dough after every rolling and sprinkling the surface with flour to prevent the rolling pin sticking and tearing the dough – put a little extra flour on the work surface as well, if required. You may think the dough is large enough, but it must be so thin that you can see the pattern in your worktop clearly (in the good old days, when caterers were allowed to use wooden boards, the dough was ready when the grain of the board was visible).

Leave the dough to rest while rolling the remaining

piece – hang it on a clean tea towel over the back of a chair or lay it on the cloth on a work surface or table. Leave for a further 10 minutes after the remaining dough is rolled.

Rolling the Dough by Machine

I am prepared to admit that I do not own either a pasta rolling pin or broom handle specifically for kitchen use. I roll my pasta by machine. These simple kitchen time-savers are a series of rollers through which the dough is passed until the required thickness is reached. Cutters for tagliatelle and spaghetti can be used, or the pasta may be left in sheets for lasagne or making into ravioli. For regular pasta eaters these machines are a worthwhile investment.

Cut the kneaded dough into six pieces about 5cm/ 2in wide and feed through the machine, starting on setting one. If you have not kneaded the dough sufficiently you may have to pass the dough through the first setting twice – you will know to do this if the surface is very rough after the first rolling; fold the dough and do it again. Continue rolling each piece of dough until the required thickness is achieved, increasing the setting of the rollers after each operation. I usually stop at setting six. Roll all pieces of dough before changing the setting of the pasta machine.

Leave the dough on a clean tea towel for about 10 minutes to dry and harden slightly before cutting. However, if you are using the strips of lasagne to make ravioli, proceed immediately, adding the filling and completing the envelopes.

Below: feed pieces of well kneaded dough through the machine on setting one, supporting it as it comes out.

Below: increase the setting of the rollers after each operation to progressively thin the dough.

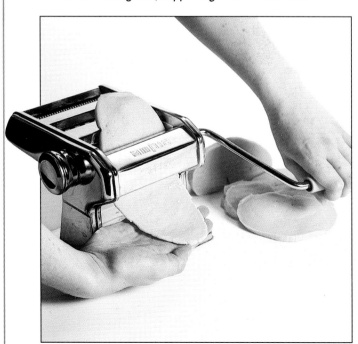

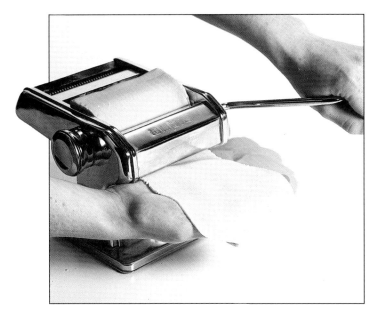

Above: it is important to support the dough as it comes out of the machine, especially as it becomes thinner.

Cutting the Dough

Roll the large circles of dough loosely and cut into thin strips about 6mm/¼inch wide, using a very sharp, flat-bladed knife. Spread the tagliatelle out carefully using your fingers – they may be cooked immediately or left until required. Wider strips may be achieved by cutting the dough, flat on a board, with a pastry-cutting wheel

Below: If cutting the dough by hand, loosely roll up the lightly floured dough.

Above: roll the dough out to the required thickness, usually setting number six.

– this will give an attractive edge to the pasta.

To cut the pasta by machine, insert the handle adjacent to either the tagliatelle or spaghetti cutters, feed the dough into the machine and turn it through the cutters, catching the shaped pasta at the other end. Spread the pasta out on the tea towel and cook immediately or when required.

Below: using a very sharp flat-bladed knife, cut the dough into 6mm/¼inch strips.

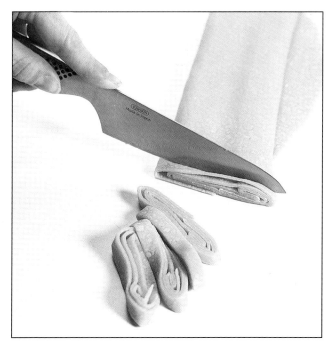

Left and below: to cut pasta by machine, into either spaghetti or tagliatelle, insert the handle into the appropriate slot adjacent to the cutter. Feed in the pasta, turning it through the cutters. Catch the strips as they come out the other side of the machine to prevent them from breaking. Wider strips or different shapes may be achieved by cutting the dough on a flat board using a pastry-cutting wheel, which also gives an attractive frilly edge to the finished pasta. Spread the pasta out on a tea-towel, or drape strips such as tagliatelle over the handle of a wooden spoon. You can cook the finished pasta immediately, or rest it until required.

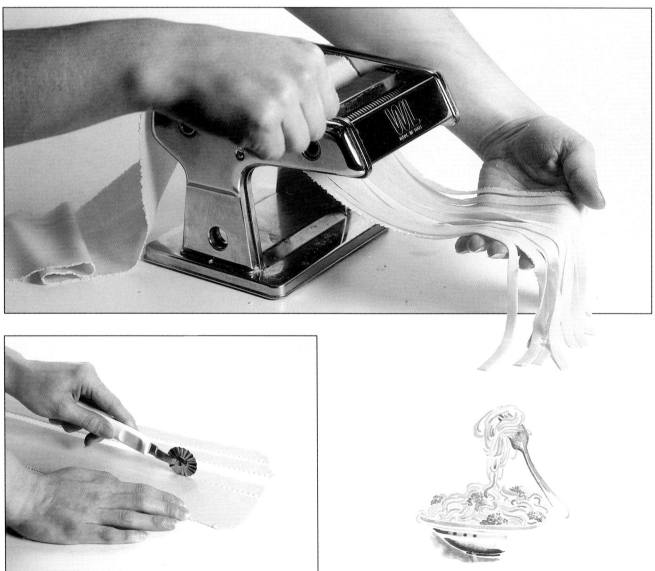

Pasta Making Attachments

The roller type of machine described above is the most common domestic pasta maker, but owners of certain table-top food preparation machines may be able to buy a pasta making attachment to use with their mixers. The pasta is prepared following a specific recipe which uses plain flour in the mixing bowl of the machine. The dough (drier than for standard pasta preparation) is ready when it forms into crumbs – not a ball as for the methods described above – and it is then fed in small pieces about the size of a hazelnut into the pasta attachment. This is locked onto the front of the machine and extrudes the pasta into the required shape. There are six screens to choose from, making this more versatile than the roller-type pasta maker. Small and large macaroni, spaghetti, rigatoni, tagliatelle and a very small lasagne – really a lasagnette without the ruffled edge – may all be made in this way. The main disadvantage of the pasta attachment is that it takes a considerable time to extrude enough pasta for six people – about 20 minutes – which may be a similar time to rolling the dough by hand but you will have the noise of a kitchen machine running throughout the extrusion process.

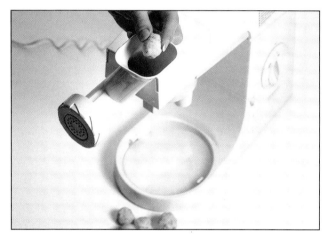

Right and below: if using a food mixer that has pasta making attachments, follow the specific recipe supplied for making pasta in the machine. The dough is fed into an extruder attachment, which with several screens makes it possible to make six different shapes.

COOKING PASTA

Boiling

The golden rule when boiling pasta is to use a large enough saucepan with plenty of water. Cooking in too small a pan causes the strands to stick together.

Always salt the cooking water – this brings out the flavour and is better than adding salt to home-made pasta dough, which occasionally makes it slightly tough. Have the water at a really fast, rolling boil before adding the pasta, which should be introduced to the pan a little at a time, stirring as more pasta is added to the water. Some people add oil to the water to help prevent the strands sticking together, but real success in keeping the pasta separate is achieved by the correct size of pan.

Boil the pasta until cooked, following directions on the packet for commercial pastas (8-15 minutes, depending on size and shape), or allowing about 3-4 minutes for fresh pasta. I never cover the pan while the pasta is cooking as it tends to make the water boil over – it is much easier to keep an eye on an open pan.

Is the Pasta Cooked?

Judging when fresh pasta is cooked is a relatively easy task as it floats to the top of the pan when ready. However, as a general rule for fresh or dried pasta, I usually scoop out a strand and test it myself – a cook's perk! Most people like their pasta "al dente" – with a little bite left in it so that it is not too soft and soggy. It is said that pasta thrown against the kitchen wall will stick when it is cooked al dente – it is up to you to evaluate the state of your kitchen decor before you try this simple test! Some people do like a firmer pasta than "al dente" and this is referred to as "fil de ferro" – "wire".

Turn the pasta into a colander but do not shake too much – over-zealous draining also encourages the pasta to stick together. Shake thoroughly the instant before serving or adding to a sauce. If the pasta is to be served plain as an accompaniment to meat, fish or, for example, a goulash, add several knobs of softened butter to coat the pasta and help to keep the strands separate – if your diet will allow.

Baking

The most commonly baked pasta is lasagne, and there are two types of dried lasagne, one of which requires par-boiling before baking, the other being used straight from the packet. The easy-cook variety should be used with a much wetter sauce than usual, to provide extra moisture for the pasta to soak up during cooking, making it less like pieces of cardboard in the finished dish. Italian easy-cook lasagne is difficult to find in the shops but gives a better result than that produced elsewhere, but there is no comparison to the sheets that have been boiled before baking.

Cook the lasagne, two or possibly three sheets at a time, according to the size of your pan, for 10-15 minutes for dried pasta and 5 minutes for fresh. Drain and lay on a clean towel until required. Cooking too many sheets at once will cause them to stick together and give great wedges of pasta in your finished dish.

Once the lasagne has been layered in an ovenproof dish with meat or vegetable sauce, finishing with a thick layer of bechamel and a good sprinkling of cheese, bake in a preheated oven at Gas Mark 4-5/180-190°C/350-375°F for about 30-40 minutes. Do not over-cook, or the edges of the top layer of lasagne will start to dry out and get crispy. No-cook lasagne is generally baked at Gas Mark 6/200°C/400°F.

Cannelloni is the other popular pasta shape for baking – large tubes made to take an ample amount of delicious filling before being cooked in the oven. Home-made cannelloni is shaped from small rectangles of pasta, about 7.5x10cm/3x4in, which are boiled, drained and then spread with a filling before being rolled up, placed in a dish and baked, either topped with melted butter or a sauce. A light, fresh-flavoured filling made from fish or vegetables (my favourite is a little smoked haddock with chopped broccoli and hard-boiled egg) is more suitable for cannelloni than a rich, meaty stuffing, which can make the dish very heavy and indigestible. You may have to visit a delicatessen or Italian grocery to find this type of pasta, which may be referred to as "pasta ripieni", simply meaning "stuffed".

Cooking Pasta in Soup

The Italian term for this method of cooking pastini is "in brodo", literally "in soup". One of the most famous Italian soups, minestrone, calls for broken spaghetti or spaghettini (very thin spaghetti) which is added once the haricot beans and vegetables are well cooked through. Pastini can be used in thick or thin soups – use more in a clear, consomme-type than in a thicker variety, which may become too filling for a starter. Chicken Noodle is a popular Chinese soup which includes pasta.

Fresh Herbs for Cooking with Pasta

If you have a garden or a window box and are fond of pasta, there are a few herbs which are easy to grow and will give your dishes wonderfully authentic flavours.

Just as kneading your own dough increases your anticipation of the meal to follow, chopping fresh herbs, especially straight from the garden, really gets the gastric juices flowing.

Fresh herbs are available in supermarkets, either in packets or in small growing pots – the pots last about 10 days if purchased very fresh and are a convenient way of having fresh herbs to hand if you are unable to grow them in full-size pots. The following are my favourites:

Parsley – preferably the flat-leaved Italian or French varieties, which have a markedly stronger flavour than the typical English curled or moss parsley. Parsley seeds germinate more readily if soaked overnight before planting – it is said that parsley only grows where a woman is dominant, so check your inter-personal skills if your parsley is either always successful or always a failure!

Basil is the most commonly used herb in Italian cookery – it has the most amazing affinity with tomatoes, which are also extensively used in the nation's cuisine. Basil will only survive outside in the warmest of summers, so is best grown in either a greenhouse or on the window-sill. Basil should be torn rather than chopped as it bruises very easily and this taints the flavour. Purple basil is a Mediterranean variety and is much more pungent in flavour than the more common green varieties.

Oregano grows wild on hillsides throughout Italy and other parts of Europe as far north as the UK. Southern Italians use oregano extensively on their pizzas – it combines well with anchovies and olives. It is also used with basil in canned and bottled Italian tomato products, for extra flavouring.

Sage grows into a large bush and would have to be grown in the garden rather than on a windowsill. It is delicious when used to flavour stuffings for cannelloni and ravioli, which may then be served with a little melted sage butter poured over, rather than the more traditional tomato-based sauces.

Remember, if you have no fresh herbs and wish to substitute dried, use 1tsp dried herbs in place of 1tbsp freshly chopped.

Sauces and Accompaniments for Pasta

One of the quickest, cheapest and most traditional sauces to serve with pasta is a tomato sauce. Simple to make at home, it tastes so much better than any commercially prepared sauce.

BASIC TOMATO SAUCE

Serves 6 people

3 tbsps olive oil
1 large onion, finely chopped or sliced
1-2 cloves garlic, finely sliced or crushed
2x425g/15oz cans chopped tomatoes –
preferably Italian
salt and freshly ground black pepper
1 tbsp freshly chopped parsley, basil or oregano

1 Heat the oil in a large frying pan, add the onion and cook slowly for at least 5 minutes, until the onion is soft but not browned.
2 Add the remaining ingredients, keeping a few herbs back for garnish. Bring to the boil, then simmer for 15-20 minutes until reduced and thickened. The cooking time for the sauce will depend very much on the quality of the canned tomatoes that you use – really thick chopped tomatoes may only require 10 minutes cooking time.
3 Season to taste with extra salt and pepper, if required, add to cooked pasta, tossing thoroughly, then serve immediately.

You might like to use fresh tomatoes when they are plentiful in the garden or cheap in the market. Allow 1 kilo/2 lbs of tomatoes for the sauce above – it would be best to skin and seed them before chopping and adding them to the pan, but I personally hate skinning tomatoes.

Above and facing page: the most traditional sauce to accompany pasta is the tomato sauce. A basic tomato sauce is so simple to make yourself and will taste so much better than any commercially prepared sauce. Start by sautéing onion, then add garlic and chopped canned tomatoes. Season with salt and pepper and chopped fresh herbs such as parsley, basil or oregano. The exact cooking time will depend on the quality of the canned tomatoes used. Fresh tomatoes can also be used, but need to be skinned, seeded and chopped first. Add the sauce to cooked, well drained pasta and toss it together thoroughly, using two forks, to ensure even coating. Serve the finished dish immediately and garnish with a little chopped fresh herbs or a herb sprig that was reserved from the tomato sauce.

Not all accompaniments to pasta are strictly sauces, inasmuch as they do not have much of a cooking period divorced from the actual pasta. I once edited a book of celebrities' recipes for a charity and received at least four versions of Spaghetti Carbonarra, a wonderful concoction of ham or bacon and lightly cooked eggs. The following recipe is foolproof:

SPAGHETTI ALLA CARBONARA

Serves 4–6

450g/1lb spaghetti, I prefer to use really thin strands
25g/1oz butter
1tbsp olive oil
125g/4oz smoked ham or bacon, chopped
4 fresh eggs, beaten
salt and freshly ground black pepper
50-75g/2-3oz freshly grated Parmesan cheese

1 Cook the spaghetti in plenty of boiling water until just al dente, then drain.
2 Meanwhile, heat together the butter and oil in a large pan, add the bacon or ham and cook for 3–4min until hot.
3 Add the drained spaghetti to the pan, mixing the ham evenly throughout the pasta.
4 Pour the eggs over the pasta, adding salt and black pepper to taste. Stir carefully over a gentle heat until the eggs are very slightly thickened. Stir in about half the Parmesan and leave the eggs to set gently in the heat from the spaghetti.
5 Serve immediately, sprinkled with the remaining cheese.

Above: add half the Parmesan to the carbonara mixture and heat through until the eggs have thickened. Sprinkle the dish with more cheese before serving for maximum flavour.

One of the surest ways of being able to prepare an excellent meal in next to no time is always to keep a jar of pesto in the cupboard. This versatile sauce can be stirred into freshly cooked pasta by the spoonful (do not heat it otherwise the oils will start to run) and a delicious meal is ready instantly – well, in as long as it has taken you to cook the pasta, which is seldom long enough to heat the plates!

Pesto (which literally means pounded) is also a versatile cooking ingredient – a spoonful makes all the difference to a minestrone or a roast pepper salad. Its one drawback is that it is expensive both to make and to buy if you want good quality, authentic ingredients – and I don't think it is worth skimping on such a gastronomic delight. The sauce, which originates from Northern Italy around Genoa, should be made with olive oil, pine nuts, garlic, fresh basil, Parmesan and pecorino cheeses and nothing else. Always check the ingredients in a commercially-prepared sauce – many contain sunflower or corn oil, peanuts instead of pine nuts, parsley and basil, and a surprising variety of cheeses. There is one affordable pesto, made in Wales, which has a good fresh flavour despite some unusual ingredients, like apple juice, but you cannot beat the following recipe:

PESTO ALLA GENOVESE

Serves 8 as a starter

125g/4oz fresh basil leaves, torn
into small pieces
½ tsp salt
½ tsp freshly ground black pepper
3-4 cloves garlic, chopped or crushed
50g/2oz pine kernels
40g/1½ oz freshly grated Parmesan
40g/1½ oz freshly grated pecorino
300ml/10fl oz extra virgin olive oil (approx)

1 Chop all the dry ingredients together in a liquidiser or food processor, then gradually add the olive oil to make a smooth paste.

2 If there is no liquidiser or food processor available, pound the dry ingredients in a pestle and mortar, then gradually stir in the oil.

3 Stir the pesto into freshly cooked pasta, but do not heat. Serve immediately.

4 Store any remaining pesto in the refrigerator for up to a week.

Note: It is the pine nuts that cause pesto to deteriorate rapidly as they can easily become rancid. Always buy pine nuts from a shop that has a rapid turnover of stock.

Left and this page: Pesto is simple to make yourself and tastes much better than many sauces that are commercially produced. The most important point is to use good quality ingredients – the freshest basil and pine nuts and your favourite olive oil, or the best quality available. Simply chop all the dry ingredients in a food processor or liquidiser, then slowly add the olive oil. The other alternative, in fact the traditional method, is to pound the dry ingredients together in a pestle and mortar and add the oil by gradually blending it in. Pesto requires no cooking whatsoever, so all you need do is stir it into your chosen cooked, drained pasta and it is ready to serve.

Cheeses to Serve with Pasta

The best known of all Italian cheeses, famous for being "sprinkled generously on" or "served with" so many pasta dishes, is Parmesan. Correctly known as "Parmigiano Reggiano", this hard cheese (formaggi di granna – hard grainy cheese) is made in the Emilia-Romagna region of Northern Italy – the gastronomic centre of the country – in an area based around the town of Parma, also famed for its hams.

Parmesan has the words "Parmigiano Reggiano" stamped on its rind and is never sold before it is two years old. Extra mature Parmesan is sold between four and five years after making. The cheese is only made from 15th April to 11th November, when the quality of the milk is just right. A trained cheese maker can tell when his product is mature and ready to sell by hitting it with a cheese hammer and hearing a very distinctive thump – like tapping the bottom of home-made bread to see if it is cooked.

Freshly cut, two-year-old Parmesan is moist and easy to cut with an ordinary kitchen knife – it makes a very good table cheese. The cheese should be kept well wrapped in the refrigerator to prevent it drying out during storage – properly wrapped it will keep for several months. Because of the very high price of Parmesan, it is unlikely that the product you have liberally sprinkled over your meal in an Italian restaurant is pure Parmigiano Reggiano. The difference in flavour between the freshly grated cheese and that sold in drums is like the difference between night and day – be warned, once you have bought a piece of the fresh cheese to grate yourself you will never want to buy a tub again!

Pecorino

This is the second most popular cheese for use with pasta and is very similar to Parmesan, except that it is made from ewe's milk and not cow's. It is unusual for ewe's milk cheeses to be cheaper than cow's milk alternatives, but this cheese is ready for sale only eight months after making, so storage and labour costs are much lower than for the two-year-old Parmesan. The cheese is made in central and southern Italy and Sardinia and has a sharp, distinctive flavour. I like to mix it with Parmesan for pesto and sometimes use it for baked dishes such as lasagne.

Mozzarella

Mozzarella is more likely to be used in salads or on pizzas than in pasta cookery. However, you might occasionally find some smoked mozzarella, which should encourage you to cancel all other recipe plans in favour of a lasagne topped with this unusual cheese – delicious!

Right: hard Italian cheeses such as Parmesan are perfect for sprinkling on pasta, pecorino can be used for sprinkling or baking, and mozzarella is perfect as a grilled topping.

Does Pasta Make You Podgy?

This is the 64-million-lire question! And I firmly believe the answer to be "no" – pasta by itself is not fattening (unless you eats loads of it every day) but it is all down to what you have with it. This is just the same as for potatoes – by themselves they are good for you – smothered in melted butter or roasted in oil they are delicious, but far more fattening.

The typical nutritive value of 100g of uncooked, dried pasta is:

Energy	1320kj (320kcal)
Protein	11.5g
Fat	1.5g
Carbohydrate	68g

This compares with the following values for commercially-prepared fresh pasta, given for 100g weights when cooked:

Energy	601kj (141kcal)
Protein	4.9g
Fat	1.4g
Carbohydrate	29.1g

As you will see, the cooked fresh values are about half the dried values, showing how pasta almost doubles in weight during cooking. Notice, however, that the fat content of the fresh pasta is higher, because of the egg content.

If dieting strictly and weighing all foods it would be better to use dried pasta – the cooked fresh would go cold while you were weighing it!

The average helping of either dried or home-made pasta is around 75-125g/3-4oz per person. If dieting very strictly you might reduce that to 50-75g/2-3oz, but if you make your sauce with very little or no oil, with chicken or fish rather than minced beef, and plenty of vegetables, you will produce a satisfying and nutritionally sound meal that you will enjoy, even if it is diet food! Serve with a salad to make a banquet.

There has been much debate throughout history as to the consequences of eating pasta. A sixteenth-century Italian doctor recommended that it should be eaten only occasionally, just with pepper and the bitter aromatic herb rue, to prevent infectious diseases, whilst a Fascist poet in the 1930s damned pasta's nutritive qualities as deceptive, claiming they induced "scepticism, sloth and pessimism". I personally would put that down to red wine in the sunshine at lunchtime!

Pastas From Around the World

Most of the pasta that I have discussed is made from wheat flour. There is, however, a useful alternative for anyone allergic to gluten, in the form of buckwheat pasta, available in good healthfood shops. Buckwheat is quite widely used in Japan for pastas and noodles.

Noodles is a generic term throughout Europe for stranded, pasta-like dough. The main difference between these and Italian pasta is that they usually contain egg, and are therefore referred to as egg noodles, whereas commercial pasta often contains no egg at all. They are often sold in compressed blocks, having been pre-steamed before packing, and these require less cooking than regular pasta.

I particularly enjoy Indonesian Mie noodles, which are made from a pasta-type dough, rolled very thinly. Such noodles are commonly used in Far Eastern cuisines.

The Chinese use egg-thread noodles extensively in

their cooking, which simply have to stand in boiling water for about 4 minutes before being drained and used.

Rice Noodles are also common in Chinese cooking, simply because rice is more widely grown in China than wheat. The usual shapes resemble spaghetti and tagliatelle, but, instead of being cut like Italian pasta, the strands are simply folded over before being dried and packaged. Rice noodles may be as thin as a vermicelli.

Chinese Cellophane Noodles are not produced through Eastern attempts to recycle unwanted packaging materials! The noodles are almost transparent (hence the name) and are made from a paste of mung-bean starch. They are often soaked before being stir-fried, rather than boiled.

Japanese Menrui is the general name given to noodles made of either white wheat or golden buckwheat. They are produced in varying thicknesses, taking anything from 7-20 minutes to cook when used straight from the packet, and are eaten soft rather than al dente. Pre-soaked noodles require slightly less cooking time, and soaking is often carried out if the noodles are to be stir-fried rather than boiled, as for the Chinese cellophane noodles.

Chapter 1

Soups
&
Appetizers

SERVES 4-6

TOMATO SOUP

An old favourite is made even more special with the addition of pasta.

30g/1oz butter or margarine
1 small onion, peeled and chopped
1 small green pepper, cored, seeds removed, and
  chopped
1 tbsp flour
1 litre/2 pints brown stock, or water plus 2 beef stock
  cubes
450g/1lb tomatoes, chopped
2 tbsps tomato purée
Salt and pepper
120g/4oz short-cut macaroni
1 tbsp grated horseradish

Garnish
2 tbsps soured cream
1 tbsp chopped parsley

Step 2 Add stock, tomatoes and tomato purée.

Step 4 Add macaroni 10 minutes before serving.

Step 2 Add flour to the onions and green pepper.

2. Add the flour and stir. Add stock, tomatoes and tomato purée. Simmer for 15 minutes.

3. Purée soup and pass through a sieve. Return to pan, and season with salt and pepper to taste.

4. Add macaroni 10 minutes before serving. Simmer and stir occasionally.

1. Heat the butter in a pan. Add the onion and green pepper, cover and cook for 5 minutes.

5. Add horseradish before serving. Garnish with soured cream and parsley. Serve immediately.

Cook's Notes

 Time
Preparation takes 15 minutes, cooking takes 45 minutes.

 Variation
Use your favourite pasta shape but ensure it is cooked through before serving the soup.

SERVES 4

MEATBALL SOUP

Kids and adults alike will enjoy this satisfying soup.

450g/1lb beef bones
1 carrot, peeled
1 onion, peeled and chopped
1 stick celery, chopped
1 egg, beaten
225g/8oz minced beef
60g/2oz breadcrumbs
Salt and pepper
1 tbsp oil
400g/14oz can plum tomatoes
175g/6oz soup pasta
1 tbsp chopped parsley

Step 2 Mix together egg, breadcrumbs and mince.

Step 3 Roll mixture into small balls and place on a roasting tin.

1. Place bones, peeled carrot, onion and celery in a large saucepan and cover with cold water. Bring to the boil: cover and simmer for 1½ hours.

2. Meanwhile, mix together lightly beaten egg with minced beef, breadcrumbs and plenty of seasoning.

3. Roll a teaspoon amount of the mixture into small balls until all the mixture is used, and place on a roasting tin with the oil. Bake in a preheated oven at 180°C/350°F/ Gas Mark 5 for 45 minutes, turning occasionally.

4. Strain stock into a saucepan. Push tomatoes and their juice through sieve, and add to stock. Bring to the boil, and simmer for 15 minutes.

5. Add pasta to the stock and cook for 10 minutes, stirring frequently.

6. Add meatballs, adjust seasoning, and stir in chopped parsley. Serve hot.

Cook's Notes

Time
Preparation takes 10 minutes, cooking takes 1 hour 40 minutes.

Variation
If you cannot buy the beef bones, cook the vegetables in beef stock for about 30 minutes.

Cook's Tip
Buy lean minced beef to keep the fat content down.

SERVES 4

RAVIOLI SOUP

Fresh pasta rectangles are filled with Parma ham and butter, then cooked in chicken stock. A tasty and filling starter for that extra special meal.

225g/8oz pasta dough (see recipe for Meat Ravioli)
3 slices Parma ham, cut into very thin strips
1lt/1¾ pints chicken stock
30g/1oz butter
1 egg, beaten
1 sprig tarragon, leaves stripped off and cut into thin strips
2 tbsps single cream
Nutmeg
Salt and pepper

Step 2 Place a little butter and Parma ham on one half of each rectangle.

1. Roll the pasta dough very thinly, either with a rolling pin or by passing through a pasta machine, and cut into rectangles.

2. Place a little Parma ham and butter on one half of each rectangle.

3. Brush the edges of each piece of dough with the beaten egg.

Step 3 Brush the edges with beaten egg.

4. Fold each rectangle in half to form a square and pinch the edges well with your fingers to seal. Cut into squares or various shapes using a ravioli cutter and pinch the edges to seal, if necessary.

5. Bring the stock to the boil, and season with nutmeg, salt and pepper.

6. Tip the ravioli into the stock and cook for approximately 2 to 5 minutes, depending on the thickness of the ravioli.

Step 4 Cut into squares or various shapes using a ravioli cutter.

7. Stir the cream into the soup just before serving and sprinkle over the tarragon. Serve hot.

Cook's Notes

Time
Preparation takes about 40 minutes (if you have just made the pasta dough, it should rest for 30 minutes in the fridge before rolling) and cooking time is approximately 10 minutes.

Cook's Tip
The use of cream in the soup is optional, but it gives a nice smooth taste to the stock.

Watchpoint
The cooking of the ravioli in the soup should be done on a very gentle simmer – the ravioli may burst open if soup boils vigorously.

SEQ 9100 JOB CLB7333-001-009 PAGE-0013 IMPORT
REVISED 17FEB93 AT 16:08 BY TF DEPTH: 66.05 PICAS WIDTH 43.04 PICAS

SERVES 4-6

BEAN SOUP

Serve this hearty soup with chunks of crusty bread and it becomes almost a meal in itself.

430g/15oz can kidney beans
60g/2oz bacon, rind removed, and chopped
1 stick celery, chopped
1 small onion, peeled and chopped
1 clove garlic, crushed
1 tbsp chopped parsley
1 tsp basil
90g/3oz can plum tomatoes, chopped and seeds
   removed
1 litre/2 pints water
1 chicken stock cube
Salt and pepper
120g/4oz wholemeal pasta

1. Place kidney beans, bacon, celery, onion, garlic, parsley, basil, tomatoes and water in a large pan. Bring to the boil and add stock cube and salt and pepper to taste.

2. Cover and cook over a slow heat for about 1½ hours.

3. Raise heat and add pasta, stirring well.

4. Stir frequently until pasta is cooked but still firm – about 10 minutes. Serve immediately.

Step 1 Place beans, bacon, celery, onion, garlic, parsley, basil and tomatoes in a large pan.

Step 3 Add pasta to pan.

Cook's Notes

Time
Preparation takes 15 minutes, cooking takes 1 hour 45 minutes.

Variation
Use a mixture of beans such as flageolets and cannellini instead of the kidney beans.

Buying Guide
Wholemeal pasta is available in lots of different shapes, buy whichever one you like best.

SERVES 4-6

MINESTRA

Spinach and herbs add a special flavour to this pasta soup.

1 onion
1 carrot
1 stick celery
30ml/2 tbsps olive oil
1½ litres/3 pints water
Salt and pepper
225g/8oz fresh spinach
2 tomatoes
120g/4oz short-cut macaroni
2 cloves garlic, crushed
2 tbsps chopped parsley
1 tsp rosemary
60g/2oz Parmesan cheese, grated

Step 4 Add chopped spinach to soup.

Step 5 Add macaroni, tomatoes and parsley to soup.

Step 1 Cut onion, carrot and celery into thin strips.

1. Cut onion, carrot and celery into thick matchstick strips.

2. Heat oil in a large, heavy pan, and fry vegetable strips until just browning, stirring occasionally.

3. Pour on water, add salt and pepper, and simmer for 20 minutes.

4. Meanwhile, wash and cut spinach leaves into shreds, add to soup and cook for 10 minutes.

5. Scald and skin tomatoes, and chop roughly, removing seeds. Add tomatoes, macaroni, garlic, parsley and rosemary to the soup, and simmer a further 10 minutes.

6. Adjust seasoning. Serve with grated Parmesan cheese if desired.

Cook's Notes

Time
Preparation takes 15 minutes, cooking takes 45 minutes.

Cook's Tip
Fresh spinach is best for this recipe, but if you only have frozen, ensure it is defrosted and well drained before using.

Watchpoint
Use freshly grated Parmesan as the pre-packaged variety will spoil the flavour of this delicate soup.

SERVES 4

CABBAGE AND PASTA SOUP

Chicken stock flavoured with bacon, cabbage, pasta and
garlic is the base for this light and tasty starter.

6 leaves white cabbage
150g/5oz small shell pasta
1 rasher streaky bacon, cut into small dice
1 clove garlic, chopped
1 tbsp olive oil
750ml/1½ pints chicken stock
Salt and pepper

1. Cut the cabbage into thin strips. To do this, roll the leaves into cigar shapes and cut with a very sharp knife.

2. Heat the olive oil and fry the garlic, bacon and cabbage together for 2 minutes.

3. Pour over the stock, season with salt and pepper and

cook on a moderate heat for 30 minutes.

4. Add the pasta to the soup after it has been cooking for 15 minutes.

5. Check the seasoning and serve.

Step 3 Pour over the stock.

Step 1 Cut the cabbage into thin strips.

Step 4 Add pasta to soup after 15 minutes cooking time.

Cook's Notes

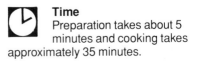 **Time**
Preparation takes about 5 minutes and cooking takes approximately 35 minutes.

 **Serving Idea**
Sprinkle over a little grated Parmesan cheese just before serving the soup.

 Variation
Leave the piece of bacon whole and remove before serving the soup.

SERVES 4

SHELL PASTA WITH TARAMASALATA

A healthy dish perfect as a starter.

Taramasalata
225g/8oz white bread, crusts removed
60ml/4 tbsps milk
225g/8oz smoked cod roe
Half an onion, grated
90ml/6 tbsps olive oil
2 tsps lemon juice
Black pepper

225g/8oz shell pasta
2 tbsps lemon juice
1 tbsp black caviar or lumpfish roe
10 black olives, pips removed and chopped

Step 6 Sprinkle lemon juice over cooked pasta.

1. To make taramasalata, crumble bread into a bowl and add milk. Set aside to soak.

2. Scoop the cod roe out of its skin, and break it down with a wooden spoon.

3. Squeeze the bread dry in a sieve. Add onion and bread to cod roe, and mix well.

4. Add oil and lemon juice very gradually, alternating between the two. Beat until smooth and creamy. Add pepper to taste, and salt if necessary.

5. Cook pasta shells in lots of boiling, salted water for 10 minutes or until *al dente*. Rinse in hot water, and drain well.

6. Sprinkle over lemon juice; toss together with taramasalata, and garnish with caviar and black olives. Serve immediately.

Step 6 Toss pasta and taramasalata together.

Step 6 Garnish with caviar and black olives.

Cook's Notes

 Time
Preparation takes 15 minutes, cooking takes 15 minutes.

 Cook's Tip
If you are in a hurry buy ready-prepared taramasalata.

SERVES 4

MACARONI WITH OLIVE SAUCE

Macaroni is served here with butter, garlic and finely chopped olives. A very tasty dish that makes an ideal starter.

300g/11oz macaroni
10 olives, green and/or black, finely chopped
1 clove garlic, finely chopped
60g/2oz butter
Salt and pepper

Step 3 Add the cooked macaroni to the garlic and olives.

Step 2 Cook garlic and olives in the butter.

1. Cook the macaroni to your liking in salted, boiling water. Rinse in hot water and set aside to drain.

2. Melt the butter in a saucepan and add the garlic and olives. Cook for 1 minute.

3. Stir in the macaroni.

4. Check the seasoning, adding salt and pepper as necessary. Serve hot.

Cook's Notes

Time
Preparation takes about 10 minutes and cooking time is approximately 20 minutes.

Variation
Add a few chopped capers to the olives, but go easy on the seasoning with salt.

Cook's Tip
Rinse the macaroni really well under hot water to prevent it from sticking together.

SERVES 4-6

FETTUCINE ESCARGOTS WITH LEEKS AND SUN-DRIED TOMATOES

6 sun-dried tomatoes or 6 fresh Italian plum tomatoes
400g/14oz canned escargots (snails), drained
340g/12oz fresh or dried whole-wheat fettucine (tagliatelle)
3 tbsps olive oil
2 cloves garlic, crushed
1 large or 2 small leeks, trimmed, split, well washed and finely sliced
6 oyster, shittake or other large mushrooms
60ml/4 tbsps chicken or vegetable stock
3 tbsps dry white wine
90ml/6 tbsps double cream
2 tsps chopped fresh basil
2 tsps chopped fresh parsley
Salt and pepper

Step 3 Properly dried tomatoes will look and feel firm, with no remaining liquid.

1. To 'sun-dry' tomatoes in the oven, cut the tomatoes in half lengthwise.

2. Use a teaspoon or your finger to scoop out about half the seeds and juice. Press gently with your palm to flatten slightly. Sprinkle both sides with salt and place tomatoes, cut side up, on a rack over a roasting tin.

3. Place in the oven on the lowest possible setting, with door ajar, if necessary, for 24 hours, checking after 12 hours. Allow to dry until no liquid is left and the tomatoes are firm. Chop roughly.

4. Drain the escargots well and dry with kitchen paper.

5. Place the fettucine in boiling, salted water and cook for about 10-12 minutes, or until al dente. Drain, rinse under hot water and leave in a colander to drain dry.

6. Meanwhile, heat the olive oil in a frying pan and add the garlic and leeks. Cook slowly to soften slightly. Add the mushrooms and cook until the leeks are tender crisp. Remove to a plate. Add the drained escargots to the pan and cook over high heat for about 2 minutes, stirring constantly.

7. Pour on the stock and wine and bring to the boil. Boil to reduce by about a quarter and add the cream and tomatoes. Bring to the boil then cook slowly for about 3 minutes. Add the herbs, salt and pepper to taste. Add the leeks, mushrooms and fettucine to the pan and heat through. Serve immediately.

Cook's Notes

 Time
Preparation takes about 24 hours for the tomatoes to dry and about 15-20 minutes to finish the dish.

 Serving Ideas
Serve as a starter or a main course with salad and bread. Grated Parmesan cheese may be sprinkled on top, if desired.

Variation
Escargots are not to everyone's taste, so substitute more mushrooms, cooked prawn or spicy sausage, as desired.

SERVES 4

TAGLIATELLE WITH SMOKED SALMON AND CAVIAR

This is the perfect way to impress your guests and you need only small amounts of the more expensive ingredients.

225g/8oz green tagliatelle
30g/1oz butter or margarine
Juice of half a lemon
Black pepper
90g/3oz smoked salmon, cut into strips
2 tbsps double cream
30g/1oz red caviar or lumpfish roe

Garnish
8 lemon slices

1. Cook tagliatelle in lots of boiling, salted water for 10 minutes, or until tender but still firm. Rinse under hot water, and drain well.

2. Heat butter in pan, and add lemon juice and freshly-

Step 2 Heat butter in a pan and add lemon juice.

Step 3 Add smoked salmon to tagliatelle and toss together.

Step 4 Serve topped with double cream and garnished with caviar.

ground black pepper.

3. Add tagliatelle to pan, and then add smoked salmon. Toss together.

4. Serve topped with double cream and a sprinkling of red caviar. Garnish with lemon slices and serve immediately.

Cook's Notes

Time
Preparation takes 5 minutes, cooking takes 15 minutes.

Cook's Tip
Red caviar is less expensive than the black variety and is easily available in supermarkets.

Watchpoint
Ensure the tagliatelle is well drained otherwise it will water down the butter sauce.

Chapter 2

Salads

SERVES 4-6

ITALIAN PASTA SALAD

This delicious-looking salad mixes some of Italy's
favourite ingredients.

450g/1lb pasta shapes
225g/8oz assorted Italian meats, cut in strips: salami,
    mortadella, prosciutto, coppa, bresaola
120g/4oz provolone or fontina cheese, cut in strips
15 black olives, halved and stoned
60g/4 tbsps small capers
120g/4oz frozen peas
1 small red onion or 2 shallots, chopped
160g/6oz oyster mushrooms, stems trimmed and sliced

Dressing
3 tbsps white wine vinegar
140ml/¼ pint olive oil
½ clove garlic, minced
1 tsp fennel seed, crushed
1 tbsp chopped parsley
1 tbsp chopped basil
1 tbsp mustard
Salt and pepper

Step 2 Add the peas to the pasta.

Step 4 Mix pasta and peas with the remaining ingredients except dressing.

Step 5 Pour dressing over salad and toss all the ingredients together.

1. Cook the pasta in a large saucepan of boiling water with a pinch of salt and 1 tbsp oil. Cook for about 10 minutes, or until just tender.

2. Add the frozen peas during the last 3 minutes of cooking time. Drain the pasta and peas and rinse under hot water. Leave in cold water until ready to use.

3. Mix the dressing ingredients together well and drain the pasta and peas thoroughly.

4. Mix the pasta and peas with the Italian meats and cheeses, olives, capers, chopped onion or shallot, and sliced mushrooms.

5. Pour the dressing over the salad and toss all the ingredients together to coat. Do not over-mix.

6. Leave the salad to chill for up to 1 hour before serving.

Cook's Notes

Time
Preparation takes 25 minutes,
cooking takes 10 minutes.

Cook's Tip
Mix the dressing ingredients
in a screw-top jar and shake
well.

Watchpoint
Don't be tempted to leave the
capers out as they add a
lovely flavour.

SERVES 4
CURRIED PRAWN SALAD

Soup pasta and prawns are mixed with a curried
mayonnaise for the perfect summer salad.

2 tbsps olive oil
1 clove garlic, crushed
1 small onion, peeled and chopped
1 level tbsp curry powder
1 tsp paprika
1 tsp tomato purée
140ml/¼ pint water
2 slices lemon
Salt
Pepper
1 tsp apricot jam
280ml/½ pint mayonnaise
225g/8oz soup pasta
Juice of ½ a lemon
225g/8oz prawns, shelled and de-veined

1. Heat oil, and fry garlic and onion gently until soft, but
not coloured.

2. Add curry powder and paprika, and cook for 2
minutes.

3. Stir in tomato purée and water. Add lemon slices, and
salt and pepper to taste. Cook slowly for 10 minutes; stir
in jam, and bring to the boil, simmering for 2 minutes.

4. Strain mixture and leave to cool. Add mayonnaise.

5. Meanwhile, cook pasta in plenty of boiling, salted
water for 10 minutes, or until tender, but still firm. Rinse
under cold water and drain well.

6. Toss pasta in lemon juice, and place in a serving-dish.
Arrange prawns on top, and pour over curry sauce. Toss
well. Sprinkle with paprika before serving.

Step 3 Stir in the
tomato purée and
water.

Step 4 Add
mayonnaise to
the strained
sauce.

Step 6 Pour
sauce over pasta
and prawns.

Cook's Notes

 Time
Preparation takes 10 minutes,
cooking takes 20 minutes.

Cooks Tip
The apricot jam adds the
slightest taste of sweetness to
the curried mayonnaise so don't be
tempted to leave it out.

 Watchpoint
Buy prawns which are fresh
and plump and have a nice
colour.

SERVES 4

BEAN SALAD

Bacon adds extra flavour to this lovely mixture of macaroni
and beans.

225g/8oz macaroni
60g/2oz bacon, rind removed, and sliced
1 onion, peeled and chopped
1-2 tbsps wine vinegar
3-4 tbsps olive oil
1 tsp chopped parsley
Salt
Pepper
425g/15oz can red kidney beans, drained
2 sticks celery, sliced diagonally

1. Cook macaroni in plenty of salted, boiling water for 10 minutes, or until tender but still firm. Rinse in cold water and drain well.

2. Heat frying pan, and sauté bacon in its own fat until

crisp. Add onion, and cook until soft.

3. Mix vinegar, oil and parsley, and season well.

4. Add bacon, onion, kidney beans and celery to macaroni.

5. Pour over dressing, and toss together.

Step 4 Add bacon, onion and kidney beans to pasta.

Step 2 Sauté bacon and add onion.

Step 5 Pour dressing over and toss to serve.

Cook's Notes

Time
Preparation takes 10 minutes, cooking takes 15 minutes.

Variation
Use smoked bacon to add extra 'bite' to the flavour.

Cooks Tip
Different onions add different flavours, try a Spanish onion for a more subtle flavour.

SERVES 6

PASTA AND VEGETABLES IN PARMESAN DRESSING

This wonderful pasta salad is colourful and delicious too.

450g/1lb pasta spirals or other shapes
225g/8oz assorted vegetables such as:
Courgettes, cut in rounds or matchsticks
Broccoli, trimmed into very small florets
Mange tout, ends trimmed
Carrots, cut in matchsticks
Celery, cut in matchsticks
Cucumber, cut in matchsticks
Spring onions, thinly shredded or sliced
Asparagus tips
French beans, sliced
Red or yellow peppers, thinly sliced

Dressing
140ml/¼ pint olive oil
3 tbsps lemon juice
1 tbsp sherry pepper sauce
1 tbsp chopped parsley
1 tbsp chopped basil
60g/2oz freshly grated Parmesan cheese
2 tbsps mild mustard
Salt and pepper
Pinch sugar

1. Cook pasta in a large saucepan of boiling, salted water with 1 tbsp oil for 10-12 minutes or until just tender. Rinse under hot water to remove starch. Leave in cold water.

2. Place all the vegetables except the cucumber into boiling, salted water for 3 minutes until just tender. Rinse in cold water and leave to drain.

3. Mix the dressing ingredients together very well.

4. Drain the pasta thoroughly and toss with the dressing. Add the vegetables and toss to coat.

5. Refrigerate for up to 1 hour before serving.

Step 2 Place vegetables in boiling salted water and cook for 3 minutes.

Step 3 Mix dressing ingredients together well.

Step 4 Toss together well to serve.

Time
Preparation takes 25 minutes, cooking takes about 15 minutes.

Cook's Tip
Try using whatever vegetables you have to hand.

Serving Idea
Serve with assorted Italian meats and French bread.

SERVES 4

MEXICAN CHICKEN SALAD

Sweetcorn and peppers add colour as well as flavour to
this attractive salad.

225g/8oz soup pasta shells
225g/8oz cooked chicken, shredded
200g/7oz can sweetcorn kernels, drained
1 stick celery, sliced
1 red pepper, cored, seeds removed, and diced
1 green pepper, cored, seeds removed, and diced

Dressing
1 tbsp mayonnaise
2 tbsps vinegar
Salt
Pepper

1. Cook pasta in plenty of boiling, salted water until just
tender. Drain well, and leave to cool.

2. Meanwhile, combine mayonnaise with vinegar and
salt and pepper to taste.

3. When the pasta is cool, add chicken, sweetcorn, celery and peppers.

4. Toss together well and serve with dressing.

Step 3 Add
chicken,
sweetcorn, celery
and peppers to
cooled pasta.

Step 2 Combine
mayonnaise,
vinegar and
seasoning.

Step 4 Toss
together well and
serve with
dressing.

Cook's Notes

 Time
Preparation takes 10 minutes,
cooking takes 15 minutes.

 Variation
Add a finely diced chilli
pepper to the dressing for a
spicy flavour.

SERVES 4

GIANFOTTERE SALAD

This interesting Italian-style salad makes the most of delicious summer vegetables.

1 small aubergine
2 tomatoes
1 large courgette
1 red pepper
1 green pepper
1 medium onion
1 clove garlic, peeled
4 tbsps olive oil
Freshly ground sea salt and black pepper
450g/1lb wholemeal pasta spirals, or bows

1. Cut the aubergine into 1cm/½-inch slices. Sprinkle with salt and leave for 30 minutes.

2. Chop the tomatoes roughly and remove the woody cores.

3. Cut the courgette into 1cm/½-inch slices.

4. Core and seed the peppers, and chop them roughly.

5. Peel and chop the onion. Crush the garlic.

6. Heat 3 tbsps olive oil in a frying pan, and fry the onion gently until it is transparent, but not coloured.

7. Rinse the salt from the aubergine thoroughly and pat dry with absorbent kitchen paper. Chop the aubergine roughly.

8. Stir the aubergine, courgette, peppers, tomatoes and garlic into the onion, and fry gently for 20 minutes. Season with salt and pepper to taste, and allow to cool completely.

9. Cook the pasta spirals in plenty of boiling salted water for 10-15 minutes, or until tender.

10. Rinse the pasta spirals in cold water and drain well.

11. Put the pasta spirals into a large mixing bowl, and stir in the remaining 1 tbsp olive oil.

12. Stir the vegetables into the pasta spirals, mixing well to make sure that they are all evenly distributed.

Step 1 Cut the aubergine into 1cm/½-inch slices. Lay the slices in a shallow dish and sprinkle with plenty of salt. Leave the aubergine for about 30 minutes to degorge.

Step 8 Add the aubergine, courgette, peppers, tomatoes and garlic to the onion in the frying pan, and cook gently for about 20 minutes.

Cook's Notes

Time
Preparation takes about 30 minutes, and cooking takes about 30 minutes.

Preparation
Degorging is the process of removing moisture from a vegetable, by sprinkling it with salt and allowing the salt to draw out the water.

Variation
If you do not have aubergines, substitute sliced mushrooms.

SERVES 6

MARINER'S SALAD

Wonderfully rich and creamy this salad is perfect for a summer picnic.

450g/1lb pasta shells, plain and spinach
4 large scallops, cleaned
280ml/½ pint frozen mussels, defrosted
140ml/¼ pint lemon juice and water mixed
120g/4oz shelled and de-veined cooked prawns
140ml/¼ pint cockles or small clams, cooked
4 crab sticks, cut in small pieces
4 spring onions, chopped
1 tbsp chopped parsley

Dressing
Grated rind and juice of ½ lemon
280ml/½ pint mayonnaise
2 tsps paprika
90ml/3 fl oz sour cream or natural yogurt
Salt and pepper

Step 4 Mix the dressing and add to the pasta.

Step 5 Toss all the ingredients together well.

Step 2 Cook scallops and mussels in the lemon and water mixture.

2. Cook the scallops and mussels in the lemon juice and water mixture for about 5 minutes, or until fairly firm.

3. Cut the scallops into 2 or 3 pieces, depending upon size.

4. Mix the dressing and drain the pasta thoroughly.

1. Cook the pasta for 10 minutes in a large pan of boiling, salted water with 1 tbsp oil. Drain and rinse under hot water. Leave in cold water until ready to use.

5. Mix all ingredients together to coat completely with dressing. Stir carefully so that the shellfish do not break-up. Chill for up to 1 hour before serving.

Cook's Notes

Time
Preparation takes 25 minutes, cooking takes 15 minutes.

Cook's Tip
The different colours of pasta are simply to make the dish prettier, so use whatever colour or shape is your favourite.

Buying Guide
Many supermarkets now sell fresh mussels at competitive prices and they have a better flavour than frozen mussels.

SERVES 4-6

TUNA AND PASTA WITH RED KIDNEY BEANS

A delicious dressing adds extra flavour to this simple, yet delicious salad.

225g/8oz small pasta shells
225g/8oz can red kidney beans, drained and rinsed
120g/4oz small mushrooms, quartered
1 can tuna, drained and flaked
4 spring onions, sliced
2 tbsps chopped mixed herbs

Dressing
140ml/¼ pint olive oil
3 tbsps white wine vinegar
Squeeze lemon juice
1 tbsp Dijon mustard
Salt and pepper

Step 4 Mix the pasta with the beans, mushrooms, tuna, spring onions and herbs.

Step 5 Pour over the dressing and toss to coat.

Step 3 Mix the dressing ingredients together.

1. Cook the pasta shells in boiling salted water with 1 tbsp oil for 10 minutes,or until just tender.

2. Rinse under hot water and then place in cold water until ready to use.

3. Mix the dressing ingredients together thoroughly. Drain the pasta shells.

4. Mix the pasta with the beans, mushrooms, tuna, spring onions and chopped mixed herbs.

5. Pour over the dressing and toss to coat. Chill up to 1 hour in the refrigerator before serving.

Cook's Notes

 Time
Preparation takes 20 minutes, cooking takes 10 minutes.

 Cook's Tip
Try to buy fresh herbs for the dressing. If you only have dried herbs halve the quantity as their flavour is stronger.

Variation
If you cannot buy the small pasta shapes substitute larger shapes such as bows or penne.

SERVES 4

MUSHROOM PASTA SALAD

Mushrooms are always delicious in a salad and this
recipe, which combines them with wholemeal pasta
shapes, is no exception.

75ml/5 tbsps olive oil
Juice of 2 lemons
1 tsp fresh chopped basil
1 tsp fresh chopped parsley
Salt and freshly ground black pepper
225g/8oz mushrooms
225g/8oz wholemeal pasta shapes of your choice

boiling water. Season with a little salt and simmer for 10 minutes, or until just tender.

5. Rinse the pasta in cold water and drain well.

6. Add the pasta to the marinated mushrooms and lemon dressing, mixing well to coat evenly.

7. Adjust the seasoning if necessary, then chill well before serving.

Step 1 Whisk the lemon juice, herbs and seasoning together in a large bowl using a fork.

Step 2 Use a sharp knife to slice the mushrooms thinly.

1. In a large bowl whisk together the olive oil, lemon juice, herbs and seasoning.

2. Finely slice the mushrooms and add these to the lemon dressing in the bowl, stirring well to coat the mushrooms evenly.

3. Cover the bowl with cling film and allow to stand in a cool place for at least 1 hour.

4. Put the pasta into a large saucepan and cover with

Step 6 Stir the cooled pasta into the marinated mushrooms, mixing well to coat evenly.

Cook's Notes

 Time
Preparation takes approximately 10 minutes, plus 1 hour at least for the mushrooms to marinate. Cooking takes about 15 minutes.

Serving Idea
Serve mushroom pasta salad on a bed of mixed lettuce.

 Variation
Use a mixture of button and wild mushrooms for a delicious variation in flavour.

SERVES 4

NIÇOISE SALAD

A classic salad which has remained a great favourite.

225g/8oz penne
200g/7oz can tuna fish, drained and flaked
3 tomatoes, quartered
½ cucumber, cut into batons
120g/4oz French beans, cooked
12 black olives, halved, with stones removed
45g/1½oz can anchovy fillets, drained, and soaked in
   milk if desired
120ml/4 fl oz bottled French dressing

Step 3 Toss pasta with tomatoes, cucumber, beans, olives and anchovies

Step 2 Put flaked tuna into the base of a serving dish.

Step 4 Pour over the French dressing.

1. Cook penne in lots of boiling, salted water until tender, but still firm. Rinse in cold water; drain, and leave to dry.

2. Put flaked tuna in the base of a salad dish.

3. Toss pasta together with tomatoes, cucumber, French beans, olives, and anchovies.

4. Pour over French dressing and mix together with the tuna.

Cook's Notes

Time
Preparation takes 15 minutes, cooking takes 15 minutes.

Cook's Tip
Soaking the anchovy fillets in milk takes away any excess saltiness.

Variation
Substitute cherry tomatoes for the large tomatoes.

SERVES 4

PRAWN SALAD

Pasta just adds that little bit extra to salads and makes them go a whole lot further too!

225g/8oz pasta shells
Juice of 1 lemon
1 tsp paprika
140ml/¼ pint mayonnaise
225g/8oz prawns, shelled and de-veined
Salt
Pepper
1 lettuce
1 cucumber, sliced

Step 3 Add mayonnaise and paprika mixture to prawns.

Step 2 Place cooked pasta in a bowl and sprinkle over lemon juice.

Step 4 Pile the prawns on top of the pasta.

1. Cook the pasta in plenty of boiling, salted water for 10 minutes, or until tender.

2. Drain, and rinse under cold water. Shake off excess water, put pasta into a bowl, and pour over lemon juice. Leave to cool.

3. Mix paprika into mayonnaise. Add to prawns, add seasoning and toss.

4. Arrange a bed of lettuce leaves and sliced cucumber in a dish, and pile pasta in centre. Pile prawns on top.

Cook's Notes

Time
Preparation takes 10 minutes, cooking takes 15 minutes.

Variation
This salad can also be made with flaked crab meat or salmon.

Serving Idea
Serve this salad on a bed of lettuce and herbs.

SERVES 4

COURGETTE SALAD

Raw vegetables are full of vitamins, and courgette in particular has a delicious taste and texture.

225g/8oz macaroni
4 tomatoes
4-5 courgettes, sliced thinly
8 stuffed green olives, sliced
90ml/6 tbsps French dressing

Step 1 Rinse the macaroni in lots of cold water, then drain well, forking it occasionally to prevent it sticking together.

1. Put the macaroni into a large saucepan and cover with boiling water. Add a little salt and simmer for 10 minutes, or until tender, but still firm. Rinse in cold water and drain well.

2. Cut a small cross in the top of each tomato and plunge into boiling water for 30 seconds.

3. Carefully remove the skins from the blanched tomatoes, using a sharp knife. Chop the tomatoes coarsely.

4. Mix all the ingredients in a large bowl and chill in the refrigerator for 30 minutes before serving.

Step 4 Mix all the ingredients together well, stirring thoroughly to blend the dressing in evenly.

Cook's Notes

Time
Preparation takes 15 minutes, cooking takes approximately 10 minutes.

Preparation
If you prefer, the courgettes can be blanched in boiling water for 1 minute, then drained and cooled before mixing with the salad ingredients.

Variation
Use any other pasta shape of your choice.

SERVES 4

TUNA AND TOMATO SALAD

Tuna and tomatoes are an ideal combination. Mix them
with basil and pasta and you have a great Italian salad.

1 tbsp chopped fresh basil
6 tbsps French dressing
340g/12oz pasta shapes of your choice
6 tomatoes
340g/12oz canned tuna fish, preferably in brine,
 drained and flaked

Step 4 Mix the pasta shapes with 3 tbsps of the French dressing in a large bowl. Stir well, to ensure that the pasta shapes are evenly coated.

1. Mix the fresh basil with the French dressing in a small jug or bowl.

2. Cook the pasta shapes in a large saucepan of boiling, lightly salted water, until they are tender. This takes about 10 minutes.

3. Rinse in cold water and drain well, shaking off any excess water.

4. Put the pasta shapes into a large bowl and toss with 3 tablespoons of the French dressing, mixing well to ensure that they are evenly coated. Leave to cool.

5. Slice enough of the tomatoes to arrange around the outside of the serving dish and then chop the rest.

6. Put the chopped tomatoes into another bowl and pour over the remaining French dressing. Put this into the

Step 7 Add the tuna to the pasta shapes and mix together gently; so that the pasta shapes are not broken.

centre of a serving dish.

7. Add the flaked tuna to the pasta shapes and toss together gently.

8. Pile the pasta shapes and tuna over the chopped tomatoes in the centre of the dish.

9. Arrange the tomato slices around the edge of the serving dish and chill well until required.

Cook's Notes

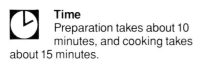

Time
Preparation takes about 10 minutes, and cooking takes about 15 minutes.

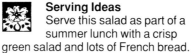

Serving Ideas
Serve this salad as part of a summer lunch with a crisp green salad and lots of French bread.

Variation
Add 2 tbsps of halved, pitted black olives for a completely different flavour.

Chapter 3

Light Meals

SERVES 2

FARFALLE WITH TOMATO SAUCE

This is a great favourite with pasta fans – simple,
delicious, and it looks good too!

1 tbsp olive oil
2 cloves garlic, crushed
1 onion, peeled and sliced
½ tsp dry basil
2 × 400g/14oz can plum tomatoes, chopped
Salt and pepper
300g/10oz farfalle (pasta bows)
2 tbsps chopped fresh basil or chopped parsley
Parmesan cheese, grated

1. Heat oil in a deep pan. Add garlic and onion, and cook until softened.

2. Add dry basil, and cook for 30 seconds.

3. Add undrained tomatoes; season with salt and pepper. Bring to the boil, reduce heat, and simmer, uncovered, for about 20 minutes, or until sauce is reduced by half.

4. Meanwhile, cook the pasta in a large pan of boiling, salted water until tender but still firm – about 10 minutes. Rinse in hot water, and drain well.

5. Push sauce through a sieve, and stir in the fresh parsley or basil.

6. Toss sauce through pasta. Serve with grated Parmesan cheese. Serve immediately.

Step 3 Add undrained tomatoes.

Step 1 Cook garlic and onion in oil until softened.

Step 5 Push sauce through a sieve.

Cook's Notes

Time
Preparation takes 10 minutes, cooking takes 30 minutes.

Buying Guide
Most supermarkets stock fresh herbs, and basil in particular, should be easy to find as it is so popular.

Cook's Tip
Tinned tomatoes with added basil will give the sauce extra flavour.

SERVES 4

PASTA SHELLS WITH SEAFOOD

Pasta and cream taste wonderful mixed with seafood in
this delicate dish.

60g/2oz butter or margarine
2 cloves garlic, crushed
75ml/5 tbsps dry white wine
280ml/½ pint single cream
1 tbsp cornflour
2 tbsps water
1 tbsp lemon juice
Salt and pepper
300g/10oz pasta shells
450g/1lb prawns, shelled and de-veined
120g/4oz scallops, cleaned and sliced
1 tbsp chopped parsley

1. Melt butter in a pan. Add garlic, and cook for 1 minute.

2. Add wine and cream, bring to the boil, and cook 2 minutes.

3. Mix cornflour with the water, and pour into sauce. Stir until boiling. Add lemon juice and salt and pepper to taste.

4. Meanwhile, cook the pasta in plenty of boiling, salted water, until tender – about 10 minutes. Drain, shaking to remove excess water.

5. Add prawns and scallops to sauce and cook 3 minutes.

6. Pour over pasta shells, toss, and garnish with parsley.

Step 5 Add prawns and scallops to the sauce.

Step 2 Add wine and cream to melted butter.

Step 6 Pour the sauce over the pasta shells to serve.

Cook's Notes

Time
Preparation takes 5 minutes, cooking takes 15 minutes.

Buying Guide
Compare the price of fresh, unshelled prawns to that of shelled and frozen prawns, as it is often better value to shell the prawns yourself.

Cooks Tip
Add a tablespoon of oil to the boiling water to prevent the pasta sticking together.

SERVES 4

SPIRALI WITH SPINACH AND BACON

Spinach is enhanced perfectly with garlic and bacon in this tasty dish.

340g/12oz pasta spirals
225g/8oz fresh spinach
90g/3oz bacon
1 clove garlic, crushed
1 small red or green chilli
1 small red pepper
1 small onion
45ml/3 tbsps olive oil
Salt and pepper

1. Cook the pasta in boiling salted water about 10-12 minutes or until just tender. Drain the pasta in a colander and rinse it under hot water. Keep the pasta in a bowl of water until ready to use.

2. Tear the stalks off the spinach and wash the leaves well, changing the water several times. Set aside to drain.

3. Remove the rind and bones from the bacon, if necessary, and dice the bacon finely. Cut the chilli and the red pepper in half, remove the stems, core and seed and slice finely. Slice the onion thinly.

4. Roll up several of the spinach leaves into a cigar shape and then shred them finely. Repeat until all the spinach is shredded.

5. Heat the oil in a sauté pan and add garlic, onion, peppers and bacon. Fry for 2 minutes, add the spinach and fry for a further 2 minutes, stirring continuously. Season with salt and pepper.

6. Drain the pasta spirals and toss them in a colander to remove excess water. Mix with the spinach sauce and serve immediately.

Step 2 Tear stalks off the spinach and wash the leaves well.

Step 3 Slice red pepper and chilli pepper in half, remove seeds and core and shred finely with a large, sharp knife.

Step 4 Roll up the leaves in several layers to shred them faster.

Cook's Notes

Time
Pasta takes about 10-12 minutes to cook. Sauce takes about 4 minutes to cook. Preparation takes about 20 minutes.

Preparation Wash spinach leaves in cold water to keep them crisp and change the water about three times to make sure all the grit is washed away.

Watchpoint
Handle chillies with care and wash hands well after chopping chillies as the juice tends to stick to the skin.

SERVES 4

PASTA PAPRIKA

An easy recipe which is delicious and quick-cooking.

340g/12oz green or wholemeal fettucine, fresh or
    dried
1 tsp sunflower oil
1 tbsp olive oil
1 large onion, chopped
1 clove garlic, crushed
3 small peppers, one green, one red and one yellow,
    seeded and sliced
450g/1lb canned tomatoes, sieved
2 tsps paprika
60g/2oz Parmesan cheese

1. Place the pasta in a large pan of boiling, salted water and add the sunflower oil. Cook for 8-15 minutes until the pasta is tender. Dried pasta will take longer to cook than fresh. Drain the cooked pasta and reserve while preparing the sauce.

2. Heat the olive oil and fry the onion, garlic and sliced peppers for about 8 minutes until softened.

3. Add the tomatoes and paprika and mix well.

4. Add the vegetable and sauce mixture to the pasta and stir well.

5. Return the mixture to a large saucepan, sprinkle over the Parmesan and heat through gently for 5 minutes. Serve immediately.

Step 4 Add the sauce and vegetable mixture to the pasta and stir well.

Cook's Notes

Time Preparation takes about 10 minutes, cooking takes about 20 minutes.	**Serving Idea** Serve as a vegetarian main course with a salad and wholemeal bread, or serve as an accompaniment to grilled chicken or fish.	**Variation** Use any combination of peppers, or all of one colour.

SERVES 4

PASTA SHELLS WITH MUSHROOM SAUCE

Pasta and mushrooms combine perfectly in this simple dish.

225g/8oz button mushrooms
30g/1oz butter or margarine
30g/1oz flour
570ml/1 pint milk
Salt and pepper
300g/10oz pasta shells

1. Rinse the mushrooms and chop them roughly.

2. Melt butter in a saucepan and add mushrooms. Fry for 5 minutes, stirring occasionally.

3. Stir in the flour and cook for 1 minute. Draw off the heat, and add milk gradually, stirring continuously. Bring to the boil and cook for 3 minutes, stirring continuously. Season with salt and pepper.

4. Meanwhile, cook the pasta shells in lots of boiling, salted water for 10 minutes, or until tender but still firm. Rinse in hot water and drain well.

5. Place in a warmed serving dish, and pour over mushroom sauce. Serve immediately.

Step 3 Gradually add milk to form mushroom sauce.

Step 1 Roughly chop the mushrooms

Step 5 Pour sauce over pasta to serve.

Cook's Notes

Time
Preparation takes 5 minutes, cooking takes 15 minutes.

Cooks Tip
Do not rinse the mushrooms too much or they will become waterlogged.

Variation
Try some of the more unusual varieties of mushroom now available in supermarkets.

SERVES 2

WHOLEMEAL SPAGHETTI WITH WALNUT AND PARSLEY

A simple recipe which makes a nice change from cheese
and tomato pasta dishes.

2 cloves garlic, peeled
60ml/4 tbsps olive oil
4 tbsps parsley
2 tbsps walnuts
3 tbsps grated Parmesan or pecorino cheese
Salt and pepper
300g/10oz wholemeal spaghetti

1. Fry garlic gently in oil for 2 minutes. Set oil aside to cool.

2. Wash parsley and remove stalks. Finely chop parsley, walnuts and garlic in a food processor with a metal blade, or in a blender.

3. When chopped well, add cooled oil in a thin stream.

4. Turn mixture into a bowl, mix in grated cheese, and

add salt and pepper to taste.

5. Cook spaghetti in a large pan of boiling, salted water for 10 minutes or until tender, but still firm. Drain.

6. Serve with sauce tossed through. Serve with a side dish of grated Parmesan or pecorino cheese.

Step 3 Add cooled oil in a thin stream.

Step 2 Finely chop parsley, walnuts and garlic in a food processor.

Step 4 Turn mixture into a bowl and mix in grated cheese.

Cook's Notes

Time
Preparation takes 10 minutes, cooking takes 10 minutes.

Cook's Tip
If you do not have a food processor simply chop the parsley, walnuts and garlic as small as possible.

Variation
If you do not like wholemeal pasta, substitute conventional spaghetti.

SERVES 4

PENNE WITH HAM AND ASPARAGUS

The Italian word penne means quills, due to the diagonal cut on both ends.

225g/8oz penne
430g/12oz fresh asparagus
120g/4oz cooked ham
30g/2 tbsps butter or margarine
280ml/½ pint double cream

Step 1 Peel the asparagus stalks with a swivel vegetable peeler.

1. Using a swivel vegetable peeler, scrape the sides of the asparagus spears starting about 5cm/2 inches from the top. Cut off the ends of the spears about 2.5cm/1 inch from the bottom.

2. Cut the ham into strips about 1.25cm/½ inch thick.

3. Bring a sauté pan of water to the boil, adding a pinch of salt. Move the pan so it is half on and half off direct heat. Place in the asparagus spears so that the tips are off the heat. Cover the pan and bring back to the boil. Cook the asparagus spears for about 2 minutes. Drain and allow to cool.

4. Cut the asparagus into 5cm/1 inch lengths, leaving the tips whole. Cut the ham into strips.

5. Melt the butter in the sauté pan and add the asparagus and ham. Cook briefly to evaporate the liquid, and add the cream. Bring to the boil and cook for about 5 minutes to thicken the cream.

6. Meanwhile, cook the pasta in boiling salted water with 15ml/1 tbsp oil for about 10-12 minutes.

7. Drain the pasta and rinse under hot water. Toss in a colander to drain and mix with the sauce. Serve with grated Parmesan cheese, if desired.

Step 4 Cut ham and cooked asparagus into 2.5cm/1 inch lengths. Leave the asparagus tips whole.

Step 5 Boil the cream with the asparagus and ham for about 5 minutes to thicken.

Cook's Notes

Time
Pasta takes 10-12 minutes to cook. Sauce takes about 8 minutes to cook. Preparation takes about 20 minutes.

Variations
If using frozen instead of fresh asparagus, do not peel or precook. Substitute broccoli spears for the asparagus and prepare in the same way. If using peas instead of asparagus, cook then in the butter with the ham, and the cream and cook 5 minutes.

Serving Ideas
May be served as a first course in smaller amounts.

SERVES 4

SHANGHAI NOODLES

In general, noodles are more popular in northern and eastern China, where wheat is grown, than in other parts of the country. Noodles make a popular snack in Chinese tea houses.

45ml/3 tbsps oil
120g/4oz chicken breasts
120g/4oz Chinese leaves
4 spring onions, thinly sliced
30ml/2 tbsps soy sauce
Freshly ground black pepper
Dash sesame oil
450g/1lb thick Shanghai noodles, cooked

Step 3 Stack up the Chinese leaves and, using a large, sharp knife, cut across into thin strips.

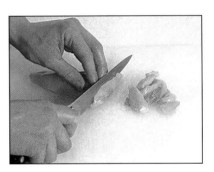

Step 1 Cut the chicken into thin strips across the grain.

Step 3 Toss in the cooked noodles, stir well and heat through.

1. Heat the oil in the wok and add the chicken cut into thin shreds. Stir-fry for 2-3 minutes.

2. Meanwhile, cook the noodles in boiling salted water until just tender, about 6-8 minutes. Drain in a colander and rinse under hot water. Toss in the colander to drain and leave to dry.

3. Add the shredded Chinese leaves and spring onions to the chicken in the wok along with the soy sauce, pepper and sesame oil. Cook about 1 minute and toss in the cooked noodles. Stir well and heat through. Serve immediately.

Cook's Notes

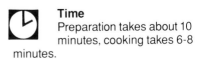

Time
Preparation takes about 10 minutes, cooking takes 6-8 minutes.

Variation
Pork may be used instead of the chicken. Add fresh spinach, shredded, if desired and cook with the Chinese leaves.

Buying Guide
Shanghai noodles are available in Chinese supermarkets and also some delicatessens. If unavailable, substitute tagliatelle or dried Chinese noodles.

SERVES 4

LASAGNE ROLLS

An interesting way of using sheets of lasagne.

2 tsps vegetable oil
8 lasagne sheets
60g/2oz button mushrooms, sliced
225g/8oz boned chicken breast
30g/1oz butter, or margarine
30g/1oz plain flour
140ml/¼ pint milk
120g/4oz Gruyère or Cheddar cheese, grated
Salt and pepper

1. Fill a large saucepan two thirds full with salted water. Add the oil and bring to the boil.

2. Add 1 sheet of lasagne, wait about 2 minutes, then add another sheet. Cook only a few at a time and when tender, after about 6-7 minutes, remove from the boiling water and rinse under cold water. Allow to drain.

3. Repeat this process until all the lasagne is cooked.

4. Wash and slice the mushrooms, and slice the chicken breast into thin strips.

5. Melt half the butter in a small frying pan and fry the mushrooms and the chicken.

6. In a small saucepan, melt the rest of the butter. Stir in the flour and heat gently for 1 minute.

7. Remove the pan from the heat and add the milk gradually to the melted butter and flour mixture, stirring well and returning the pan to the heat between additions, to thicken the sauce.

8. Beat the sauce well and cook for 3 minutes, until it is thick and smooth.

9. Pour the sauce into the frying pan with the chicken and the mushrooms. Add half the cheese and mix well to incorporate thoroughly. Season to taste.

10. Lay the sheets of lasagne on a board and divide the chicken mixture equally between them.

11. Spread the chicken mixture evenly over each lasagne sheet and roll up lengthways, like a swiss roll.

12. Put the rolls into an ovenproof dish. Sprinkle with the remaining cheese and grill under a pre-heated moderate grill, until the cheese is bubbly and golden brown.

Step 5 Melt half the butter in a large frying pan and add the mushrooms and chicken. Fry these quickly, stirring continuously until the chicken is cooked.

Step 11 Spread the chicken mixture evenly over each sheet of lasagne and roll up swiss roll fashion, starting from a narrow end.

Cook's Notes

Time
Preparation takes about 10 minutes, and cooking takes about 15 minutes.

Cook's Tip
Precooked lasagne is now widely available at most supermarkets and does not require as much initial cooking. If available, try preparing this dish with sheets of fresh lasagne, which require the least precooking of all.

Variation
For a delicious vegetarian alternative, use Stilton cheese and 120g/4oz broccoli florets, instead of the chicken breasts.

SERVES 4

HOME-MADE TAGLIATELLE WITH SUMMER SAUCE

Pasta making is not as difficult as you might think. It is well worth it, too, because home-made pasta is in a class by itself.

Pasta Dough
120g/4oz plain flour
120g/4oz fine semolina
2 large eggs
10ml/2 tsps olive oil
Pinch salt

Sauce
450g/1lb unpeeled tomatoes, seeded and cut into small dice
1 large green pepper, cored, seeded and cut in small dice
1 onion, cut in small dice
15ml/1 tbsp chopped fresh basil
15ml/1 tbsp chopped fresh parsley
2 cloves garlic, crushed
140ml/¼ pint olive oil and vegetable oil mixed

1. Combine all the sauce ingredients, mixing well. Cover and refrigerate overnight.

2. Place the flours in a mound on a work surface and make a well in the centre. Place the eggs, oil and salt in the centre of the well.

3. Using a fork, beat the ingredients in the centre to blend them and gradually incorporate the flour from the outside edge. The dough may also be mixed in a food processor.

4. When half the flour is incorporated, start kneading using the palms of the hands and not the fingers. This may also be done in a food processor. Cover the dough and leave it to rest for 15 minutes.

5. Divide the dough in quarters and roll out thinly with a rolling pin on a floured surface or use a pasta machine, dusting dough lightly with flour before rolling. If using a machine, follow the manufacturer's directions. Allow the sheets of pasta to dry for about 10 minutes on a floured surface or tea towels. Cut the sheets into strips about 5mm/¼ inch wide by hand or machine, dusting lightly with flour while cutting.

6. Cook the pasta for 5-6 minutes in boiling salted water with a spoonful of oil. Drain the pasta and rinse under very hot water. Toss in a colander to drain excess water. Place the hot pasa in a serving dish. Pour the cold sauce over and toss.

Step 4 Knead with palms of hands to bring dough together until smooth.

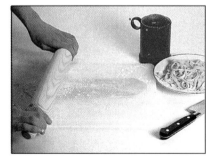

Step 5 Roll the dough out thinly and cut into thin strips.

Cook's Notes

Time
Overnight refrigeration for the sauce. Preparation time takes about 30 minutes, cooking takes about 5-6 minutes.

Watchpoint
Pasta must remain very hot to balance the cold sauce.

Serving Ideas
This basic pasta recipe can be used with other shapes of pasta such as lasagne, cannelloni, ravioli, farfalle (butterflies or bows) or cut into very fine noodles.

SERVES 4

SMOKED HADDOCK WITH PEAS AND PASTA

This colourful fish and pasta dish tastes as good as it looks.

280ml/½ pint milk
225g/8oz smoked haddock fillets
30g/1oz butter or margarine
30g/1oz flour
45g/1½oz frozen peas, cooked
1 tbsp chopped chives
1 tbsp chopped parsley
1 hard-boiled egg, chopped
Salt and pepper
225g/8oz pasta shells, cooked

1. Heat the milk gently in a large frying pan which has a tight-fitting lid. Add the fish when the milk is warm, cover the pan and poach the fish gently for about 8 minutes. Season the fish and check the pan occasionally, adding a little more milk if necessary. When ready, drain the fish, reserving the milk.

2. Melt the butter, stir in the flour and heat gently for a few minutes. Add the reserved milk, stirring continuously. Heat until sauce thickens; if it is too thick, add a little more milk.

3. Add the chives and parsley to the sauce and pour the sauce into a large bowl. Skin and flake the fish, removing any bones. Add the fish to the sauce along with the peas, hard-boiled egg and salt and pepper. Stir together well.

4. Add the drained pasta to the sauce mixture and again mix gently to distribute the fish through the pasta and sauce.

5. Return the mixture to a large saucepan and heat over a gentle heat for 3-4 minutes. Serve immediately.

Step 3 Add the peas and fish to the sauce, along with the pasta.

Cook's Notes

Time
Preparation takes about 10 minutes and cooking takes about 25 minutes.

Cook's Tip
Pasta can be cooked in a microwave oven. Combine 225g/8oz pasta shapes with 850ml/1½ pints boiling water. Cook on high for about 7-10 minutes. Cover and let it stand for 5 minutes. Drain and rinse in hot water.

Serving Idea
Serve with a tossed green salad.

SERVES 4

MEE GORENG

These "celebration stir-fry noodles" are of Indonesian
origin and are so easy to prepare that they make an ideal
quick lunch or supper dish.

225g/8oz fine egg noodles
4 tbsps peanut oil
1 onion, finely chopped
2 cloves garlic, crushed
1 green chilli, seeded and finely sliced
1 tsp chilli paste
120g/4oz pork, finely sliced
2 sticks of celery, sliced
¼ small cabbage, finely shredded
1 tbsp light soy sauce
120g/4oz prawns, shelled and deveined
Salt and pepper

Step 4 Stir-fry the pork, celery and cabbage with the onion mixture for 3 minutes, or until the pork is cooked through.

Step 1 Soak the noodles in hot water for 8 minutes, until they are soft. Rinse in cold water and drain thoroughly in a colander.

1. Soak the noodles in hot water for 8 minutes, until they are soft. Rinse in cold water and drain thoroughly in a colander.

2. Heat the oil in a wok and stir-fry the onion, garlic and chilli, until the onion is soft and just golden brown.

3. Add the chilli paste and stir in well.

4. Add the pork, celery and cabbage to the fried onions, and stir-fry for about 3 minutes, or until the pork is cooked through. Season to taste.

5. Stir in the soy sauce, noodles and prawns, tossing the mixture together and heating through before serving.

Cook's Notes

Time
Preparation takes about 20 minutes, and cooking takes about 15 minutes.

Serving Ideas
Serve with plain boiled rice and prawn crackers.

Watchpoint
Great care should be taken when preparing fresh chillies. Try not to get juice into the eyes or mouth. If this should happen, rinse well with lots of cold water.

SERVES 6

PASTA WITH FRESH TOMATO AND BASIL SAUCE

Pasta is a good item to include on a low calorie diet, as it is very filling and can be served with any variety of low calorie sauces.

1 small onion
450g/1lb fresh tomatoes
2 tbsps tomato purée
1 orange
2 cloves garlic, crushed
Salt and freshly ground black pepper
140ml/¼ pint red wine
140ml/¼ pint chicken stock
30ml/2 tbsps coarsely chopped basil
340g/12oz pasta shapes

1. Peel and finely chop the onion.

2. Cut a small cross in the skins of the tomatoes and plunge them into boiling water for 30 seconds. Remove the blanched tomatoes from the water and carefully peel away the loosened skin.

3. Cut the tomatoes into quarters, and remove and discard the pips. Chop the tomato flesh roughly, and put this, the onion and the tomato purée into a large saucepan.

4. Heat the onion and tomatoes over a gentle heat, stirring continuously until the tomatoes soften and begin to lose their juice.

5. Finely grate the rind from the orange. Cut the orange in half and squeeze out the juice.

6. Put the orange, rind and juice into a large saucepan along with all the remaining ingredients except the pasta, and bring to the boil.

Step 1 To chop an onion finely, pierce the peeled onion with a fork and use this to hold the vegetable steady whilst you chop with a sharp knife.

Step 3 Cut the tomatoes into quarters and remove and discard the seeds.

7. Continue to boil until the sauce has reduced and thickened and the vegetables are soft.

8. Whilst the sauce is cooking, put the pasta into another saucepan with enough boiling water to cover. Season with a little salt and cook for 10-15 minutes, or until the pasta is soft.

9. Drain the pasta in a colander, and stir it into the hot sauce. Serve at once with a salad.

Time
Preparation takes 15-20 minutes, cooking takes 10-15 minutes.

Variation
Add 120g/4oz thinly sliced mushrooms to the sauce, if liked.

Freezing
This sauce will freeze very well for up to 3 months.

SERVES 6

NOODLES WITH POPPY SEEDS AND RAISINS

Christmas Eve dinner in Poland traditionally had up to
21 courses, of which this was but one!

225g/8oz noodles or other pasta shapes
Pinch salt
15ml/1 tbsp oil
140ml/¼ pint double cream
90g/6 tbsps black poppy seed, ground
30ml/2 tbsps honey
90g/6 tbsps raisins

1. Bring lots of water to the boil in a large saucepan with a pinch of salt. Add the oil and the noodles or other pasta shapes and bring back to the boil. Cook, uncovered, until tender, about 10-12 minutes.

2. Drain and rinse the pasta under hot water. If using immediately, allow to drain dry. If not, place in a bowl of water to keep.

3. Place the cream in a deep, heavy-based saucepan

Step 3 Cream is at scalding point when it begins to bubble round the edges. Remove quickly from the heat, it can boil over.

Step 3 Pour the poppy seeds, honey and raisins into the cream, mixing very well.

Step 3 The poppy seed mixture should be thick when ready, but still fall from the spoon easily.

and bring almost to the boil. When the cream reaches the scalding point, mix in the poppy seeds, honey and raisins. Cook slowly for about 5 minutes. The mixture should become thick but still fall off a spoon easily. Use a food processor or spice mill to grind the poppy seeds.

4. Toss the poppy seed mixture with the noodles and serve hot.

Cook's Notes

Serving Ideas
Serve as a course on its own in a Polish Christmas Eve dinner or as a side dish to duck, pork or gammon.

Time
Preparation takes about 15 minutes and cooking takes about 15-17 minutes.

Variation
Use currants or sultanas.

SERVES 4

SPAGHETTI AMATRICIANA

This is another quickly cooked sauce with a rich spicy
taste. Use less of the chilli pepper for a less fiery flavour.

1 onion
6 strips smoked back bacon
450g/1lb ripe tomatoes
1 chilli pepper
25ml/1½ tbsps oil
340g/12oz spaghetti

1. Slice the onion thinly. Remove rind from the bacon
and cut into thin strips.

2. Drop the tomatoes into boiling water for 6-8 seconds.
Remove with a draining spoon and place in cold water,
and leave to cool completely. This will make the peels
easier to remove.

3. When the tomatoes are peeled, cut them in half and
remove the seeds and pulp with a teaspoon. Rub the
seeds and pulp through a strainer and retain juice to use
in the sauce if desired. Chop the tomato flesh roughly
and set it aside.

4. Cut the stem off the chilli pepper and cut the pepper in
half lengthways. Remove the seeds and core and cut the
pepper into thin strips. Cut the strips into small dice.

5. Heat the oil in a sauté pan and add the onion and bacon. Stir over medium heat for about 5 minutes, until the
onion is transparent. Drain off excess fat and add the
tomatoes and chilli and mix well. Simmer the sauce
gently, uncovered, for about 5 minutes, stirring
occasionally.

6. Meanwhile, cook the spaghetti in boiling salted water
with 15ml/1 tbsp oil for about 10-12 minutes. Drain and
rinse in hot water and toss in a colander to dry. To serve,
spoon the sauce on top of the spaghetti and sprinkle with
freshly grated Parmesan cheese, if desired.

Step 2 Placing
tomatoes in
boiling water and
then in cold water
makes the skins
easier to remove.

Step 3 Cut the
peeled tomatoes
in half and
remove the seeds
and pulp with a
teaspoon. Cut the
flesh roughly.

Step 4 Remove
the stems, seeds
and cores from
the chilli pepper,
cut into thin strips
and then chop
into fine dice.

Cook's Notes

Time
Spaghetti takes about 10-12
minutes to cook, sauce takes
about 8 minutes to cook, preparation
takes about 20-25 minutes.

Cook's Tip
It is not necessary to use the
whole chilli pepper; use as
much as desired.

Watchpoint
Wash hands very well after
handling chilli peppers or use
rubber gloves while chopping them.

SERVES 4

SPICY ORIENTAL NOODLES

A most versatile vegetable dish, this goes well with meat
or stands alone for a vegetarian main course.

225g/8oz Chinese noodles (medium thickness)
75ml/5 tbsps oil
4 carrots, peeled
225g/8oz broccoli
4 spring onions, diagonally sliced
12 Chinese mushrooms, soaked 30 minutes
1 clove garlic, peeled
1-2 tsps chilli sauce, mild or hot
60ml/4 tbsps soy sauce
60ml/4 tbsps rice wine or dry sherry
2 tsps cornflour

1. Cook noodles in boiling, salted water for about 4-5 minutes. Drain well, rinse under hot water to remove starch and drain again. Toss with about 1 tbsp of the oil to prevent sticking.

2. Using a large, sharp knife, slice the carrots thinly on the diagonal.

3. Cut the florets off the stems of the broccoli and divide into even-sized, but not too small sections. Slice the stalks thinly on the diagonal. If they seem tough, peel them before slicing.

4. Place the vegetables in boiling water for about 2 minutes to blanch. Drain and rinse under cold water to stop them cooking, and leave to drain dry.

5. Remove and discard the mushroom stems and slice the caps thinly. Set aside with the other vegetables.

6. Heat a wok and add the remaining oil with the garlic clove. Leave the garlic in the pan while the oil heats and then remove it. Add the carrots and broccoli and stir-fry about 1 minute. Add mushrooms and onions and continue to stir-fry, tossing the vegetables in the pan continuously.

7. Combine chilli sauce, soy sauce, wine and cornflour, mixing well. Pour over the vegetables and cook until the sauce clears. Add the noodles, toss together well to heat them through and serve immediately.

Step 7 Cook the vegetables and sauce ingredients until cornflour thickens and clears.

 Cook's Notes

 **Time** Preparation takes about 25 minutes and cooking takes about 7-8 minutes.	**Variation** If you prefer you can add meat or prawns to this recipe. Stir-fry the meat or prawns before adding the vegetables.	**Serving Ideas** Use as a side dish with chicken, meat or fish, or serve as a starter. May also be served cold as a salad.

SERVES 4

...TA SPIRALS WITH CREAMY PARSLEY SAUCE

Quick and easy to prepare, this dish is perfect for unexpected guests.

30g/1oz butter or margarine
15g/½oz flour
280ml/½ pint milk
300g/10oz pasta spirals
1 tbsp lemon juice, or ½ tbsp vinegar
1 tbsp chopped parsley

Step 1 Heat butter in a pan and when melted, stir in the flour.

1. Heat butter gently in a saucepan; when melted, stir in flour. Cook for 1 minute.

2. Remove from heat, and gradually stir in milk. Return to heat, and stir continuously until boiling. Cook for 2 minutes.

3. Meanwhile, cook pasta spirals in lots of boiling, salted water for 10 minutes, or until tender but still firm. Rinse in hot water, and drain well.

4. Add lemon juice and parsley to sauce and stir well.

5. Pour sauce over pasta and mix well. Serve immediately.

Step 4 Add lemon juice and parsley to sauce.

Step 5 Pour sauce over pasta and mix well.

Cook's Notes

Time
Preparation takes 5 minutes, cooking takes 15 minutes.

Variation
If serving this dish to children try using tri-coloured pasta spirals for a colourful meal.

SERVES 2

TAGLIATELLE WITH GARLIC AND OIL

A simple recipe which is surprisingly tasty.

300g/10oz green tagliatelle
140ml/¼ pint olive oil
3 cloves garlic, crushed
2 tbsps chopped parsley
Salt and pepper

Step 4 Add sauce to tagliatelle.

Step 2 Add garlic and parsley to warmed oil.

Step 4 Toss the pasta and sauce together well.

1. Cook the tagliatelle in lots of boiling, salted water for 10 minutes, or until tender but still firm. Stir occasionally.

2. Meanwhile, make the sauce. Heat the oil in a pan and, when warm, add peeled, crushed garlic. Fry gently until golden brown.

3. Add chopped parsley, and salt and pepper to taste.

4. Drain tagliatelle. Add sauce, and toss to coat well. Serve hot.

Cook's Notes

Time
Preparation takes 5 minutes, cooking takes 10 minutes.

Cook's Tip
Use extra virgin olive oil for this recipe as it has the best flavour.

Serving Idea
Serve this simple dish with Italian bread or with Italian meats if you want to make it a bit heartier.

SERVES 6

PASTA WITH LEEKS AND MUSSELS

This rather unusual pasta dish is relatively quick and easy to prepare.

1lb mussels
120ml/4 fl oz white wine
1 shallot, chopped
2 medium-sized leeks
180ml/6 fl oz double cream
450g/1lb spiral-shaped pasta
1 tbsp oil
2 slices ham
1½ tbsps butter
Chopped chives to garnish
Salt and pepper

Step 3 Cook leeks in the cream with salt and pepper.

1. Scrub the mussels; remove the beards and wash in several changes of water to eliminate the sand.

2. In a large, covered saucepan, cook the mussels in the white wine with the chopped shallot for approximately 5 minutes, over a high heat. Cool, and remove the opened mussels from their shells. Reserve the cooking liquid.

3. Quarter each leek lengthwise, wash thoroughly, and slice finely. In a covered saucepan, cook the leeks in the cream, with salt and pepper to taste, for 10 minutes over a low heat.

4. In a large pan of boiling water, boil the pasta with 1 tbsp oil. Stir the pasta occasionally as it cooks, to prevent sticking. Drain after 5 or 6 minutes. Rinse in cold water to prevent sticking.

5. Remove any fat or rind from the ham, and slice into small pieces.

6. Strain the mussel cooking liquid through a sieve lined with cheesecloth. Measure out approximately ½ cup.

7. Add the shelled mussels and the mussel liquid to the cream mixture, and cook for 4 minutes, stirring constantly.

8. Melt the butter in a deep frying pan, and reheat the

Step 8 Reheat pasta and add ham.

Step 9 Add leek sauce to pasta.

pasta gently with the ham. Season to taste.

9. When the pasta is heated through, add the cream and leek sauce, and serve garnished with the chopped chives.

Cook's Notes

Time
Preparation takes 30 minutes, cooking takes 25 minutes.

Cook's Tip
Use your favourite kind of ham in this dish.

SERVES 3-4

SPAGHETTI WITH TOMATO, SALAMI AND GREEN OLIVES

Salami tastes great with pasta and it is convenient too.

400g/14oz can plum tomatoes
½ tbsp oregano
150g/5oz salami, sliced and shredded
200g/7oz green olives, stoned and chopped
Salt and pepper
300g/10oz spaghetti
2 tbsps olive oil
1 clove garlic, crushed
60g/2oz pecorino cheese, grated

Step 2 Add oregano, olives and salami to tomatoes.

Step 1 Purée tomatoes and push through a sieve.

Step 5 Pour sauce over spaghetti.

1. Purée tomatoes, and push through a sieve into a saucepan.

2. Add oregano, salami and olives, and heat gently. Add salt and pepper to taste.

3. Meanwhile, cook spaghetti in plenty of boiling, salted water for 10 minutes, or until tender but still firm. Drain well.

4. Heat olive oil and add garlic and freshly-ground black pepper to the pan used to cook the spaghetti.

5. Add spaghetti to the pan, and pour the sauce over. Toss well. Serve immediately with pecorino cheese.

Cook's Notes

Time
Preparation takes 15 minutes, cooking takes 15 minutes.

Buying Guide
Buy your favourite salami or a variety of different types for this dish.

Variation
Use any other pasta shape of your choice.

Chapter 4

Main Meals

SERVES 4
RAVIOLI WITH RICOTTA CHEESE

Preparing your own pasta dough is simple and making
ravioli is good fun too!

Filling
30g/1oz butter or margarine
1 egg yolk
225g/8oz ricotta cheese
60g/2oz Parmesan cheese, grated
2 tbsps chopped parsley
Salt
Pepper

Dough
275g/9oz strong plain flour
Pinch of salt
3 eggs

Tomato sauce
1 tbsp olive oil
30g/1oz bacon
1 small onion, peeled and chopped
1 bay leaf
1 tsp basil
1 tbsp flour
400g/14oz can plum tomatoes
Salt
Pepper
1 tbsp double cream

Step 5 Shape the filling into small balls and place about 4cm/1½ inches apart on the dough.

1. To make the filling, beat the butter to a cream, add egg yolk, and blend well. Beat ricotta cheese to a cream, and add butter-egg mixture gradually, mixing until smooth.

2. Add Parmesan cheese and parsley, and salt and pepper to taste. Set aside.

3. To make the dough, sift flour in a bowl with the salt. Make a well in the centre, and add the eggs. Work flour and eggs together with a spoon, and then knead by hand until a smooth dough is formed. Leave to rest for 15 minutes.

4. Lightly flour a board, and roll dough out thinly into a rectangle. Cut dough in half.

5. Shape the filling into small balls and set them about 4cm (1½″) apart on one half of the dough. Place the other half on top and cut with a ravioli cutter or small pastry cutter. Seal the edges with a fork or the fingertips.

6. Cook in batches in a large, wide pan with plenty of boiling, salted water until tender – about 8 minutes. Remove carefully with a perforated spoon.

7. While the pasta is boiling, prepare the sauce. Heat oil, and fry bacon and onion until golden. Add bay leaf and basil, and stir in flour. Cook for 1 minute, draw off heat, and add tomatoes gradually, stirring continuously. Add salt and pepper to taste.

8. Return to heat and bring to the boil. Cook for 5 minutes, then push through a sieve. Stir in cream, and adjust seasoning.

9. Pour sauce over ravioli. Serve immediately.

Cook's Notes

Time
Preparation takes 30 minutes, cooking takes 20 minutes.

Buying Guide
Always buy fresh Parmesan and grate it yourself as its flavour is far better than ready-grated Parmesan.

Watchpoint
Remember to remove the bay leaf from the sauce before pouring over ravioli.

SERVES 2

TAGLIATELLE CARBONARA

A classic Italian favourite that is simply delicious.

1 tbsp olive oil
120g/4oz streaky bacon rashers, rind removed, and
  shredded
Pinch of paprika
60ml/4 tbsps single cream
2 eggs
60g/2oz Parmesan cheese, grated
300g/10oz tagliatelle
30g/1oz butter or margarine
Salt and pepper

3. Beat together eggs and grated cheese.

4. Meanwhile, cook tagliatelle in lots of boiling, salted water for 10 minutes, or until tender but still firm. Drain, return to pan with butter and black pepper, and toss.

5. Add bacon mixture and egg mixture, and toss together. Add salt to taste. Serve immediately.

Step 3 Beat eggs and cheese together.

Step 2 Add cream to bacon and paprika and stir.

Step 5 Toss the bacon and pasta together well.

1. Heat oil in a frying-pan, and cook bacon over a moderate heat until browning.

2. Add paprika and cook for 1 minute. Add cream, and stir.

Cook's Notes

Time
Preparation 10 minutes,
cooking takes 15 minutes.

Serving Idea
This dish is superb served
simply with an Italian bread
such as Ciabatta.

SERVES 4

CANNELLONI

This old favourite is one of the most rewarding pasta
dishes to prepare.

12 cannelloni shells
2 tbsps Parmesan cheese, grated
1 tbsp oil

Filling
1 tbsp olive oil
2 cloves garlic, crushed
1 onion, peeled and chopped
450g/1lb minced beef
1 tsp tomato purée
½ tsp basil
½ tsp oregano
225g/8oz packet frozen spinach, thawed
1 egg, lightly beaten
60ml/4 tbsps double cream
Salt and pepper to taste

Tomato sauce
1 tbsp olive oil
1 onion, peeled and chopped
1 clove garlic, crushed
400g/14oz can plum tomatoes
2 tbsps tomato purée
Salt
Pepper

Béchamel sauce
280ml/½ pint milk
1 slice of onion
3 peppercorns
1 small bay leaf
30g/1oz butter or margarine
30g/1oz flour
Salt
Pepper

1. To make the filling, heat oil in pan, and fry garlic and onion gently until soft and transparent. Add meat and cook, stirring continuously, until well browned.

2. Drain off any fat, add tomato purée, basil and oregano, and cook gently for 15 minutes.

3. Add spinach, egg and cream, and salt and pepper to taste.

4. Cook cannelloni in a large pan of boiling, salted water for 15-20 minutes, until tender. Rinse in hot water and drain.

5. Fill carefully with meat mixture, using a piping bag with a wide, plain nozzle, or a teaspoon.

6. To make tomato sauce, heat oil in pan. Add onion and garlic, and cook gently until transparent.

7. Push tomatoes through a sieve, and add to the pan with tomato purée and salt and pepper to taste. Bring to boil, and then simmer for 5 minutes. Set aside.

8. To make Béchamel Sauce, put milk in pan with onion, peppercorns and bay leaf. Heat gently for 1 minute, taking care not to boil, and set aside to cool for 5 minutes. Strain.

9. Melt butter in pan. Remove from heat and stir in flour. Gradually add cool milk, and bring to boil, stirring continuously, until sauce thickens. Add seasoning.

10. Spread tomato sauce on the base of an oven-proof dish. Lay cannelloni on top, and cover with Béchamel sauce. Sprinkle with grated cheese, and bake in a moderate oven at 180°C/350°F/Gas Mark 4 for 30 minutes. Serve immediately.

Cook's Notes

 Time
Preparation takes 10 minutes, cooking takes 1 hour.

Serving Idea
A hearty Italian red wine, such as Barolo, is good with this dish.

 Buying Guide
When buying olive oil try to buy the best quality possible – extra virgin olive oil tastes much better than a blended olive oil.

SERVES 6

LASAGNE NAPOLETANA

This is lasagne as it is cooked and eaten in Naples. With its layers of red, green and white it looks as delicious as it tastes and is very easy to prepare and assemble.

9 sheets spinach lasagne pasta

Tomato Sauce
45ml/3 tbsps olive oil
2 cloves garlic, crushed
900g/2lbs fresh tomatoes, peeled, or canned
    tomatoes, drained
2 tbsps chopped fresh basil, six whole leaves reserved
Salt and pepper
Pinch sugar

Cheese Filling
450g/1lb ricotta cheese
60g/3 tbsps unsalted butter
225g/8oz Mozzarella cheese, grated
Salt and pepper
Pinch nutmeg

1. Cook the pasta for 8 minutes in boiling salted water with 15ml/1 tbsp oil. Drain and rinse under hot water and place in a single layer on a damp cloth. Cover with another damp cloth and set aside.

2. To prepare the sauce, cook the garlic in remaining oil for about 1 minute in a large saucepan. When pale brown, add the tomatoes, basil, salt, pepper and sugar. If using fresh tomatoes, drop into boiling water for 6-8 seconds. Transfer to cold water and leave to cool completely. This will make the peels easier to remove.

3. Lower the heat under the saucepan and simmer the sauce for 35 minutes. Add more seasoning or sugar to taste.

4. Beat the ricotta cheese and butter together until creamy and stir into the remaining ingredients.

5. To assemble the lasagne, oil a rectangular baking dish and place 3 sheets of lasagne on the base. Cover with one third of the sauce and carefully spread on a layer of cheese. Place another 3 layers of pasta over the cheese and cover with another third of the sauce. Add the remaining cheese filling and cover with the remaining pasta. Spoon the remaining sauce on top.

6. Cover with foil and bake for 20 minutes at 190°C/375°F/Gas Mark 5. Uncover and cook for 10 minutes longer. Garnish with the reserved leaves and leave to stand 10-15 minutes before serving.

Step 5 Place pasta on the base of an oiled baking dish. Spread tomato sauce over.

Step 5 Carefully spread the softened cheese mixture on top of the tomato sauce.

Cook's Notes

Cook's Tip
Lasagne can be assembled the day before and refrigerated. Allow 5-10 minutes more cooking time in the oven if not at room temperature.

Time
Preparation takes about 25 minutes, cooking takes about 1-1¼ hours.

Variations
Use plain pasta instead, if desired. If using pre-cooked lasagne pasta, follow the baking times in the package directions.

SERVES 2-3

FARFALLE WITH BEEF, MUSHROOM AND SOURED CREAM

This is a great mid-week meal, especially for all those confirmed meat eaters in the family!

225g/8oz fillet or rump steak, sliced
30g/1oz unsalted butter
1 onion, peeled and sliced
120g/4oz mushrooms, sliced
1 tbsp flour
60ml/2 fl oz soured cream
10 green olives, stoned and chopped
Salt and pepper
300g/10oz farfalle (pasta bows)

Garnish
Soured cream
1 tbsp chopped parsley

1. With a very sharp knife, cut meat into narrow, short strips. Heat half the butter, and fry meat over a high heat until well browned. Set aside.

2. Heat remaining butter in pan, and gently fry onion until soft and just beginning to colour.

3. Add mushrooms, and cook for 3 minutes. Stir in flour and continue frying for a further 3 minutes.

4. Gradually stir in soured cream. When fully incorporated, add meat, olives, and salt and pepper to taste.

5. Meanwhile, cook farfalle in plenty of boiling, salted water for 10 minutes, or until tender but still firm. Drain well.

6. Serve pasta with beef and mushroom sauce on top. Garnish with a little extra soured cream and chopped parsley.

Step 1 Cut beef into narrow strips.

Step 3 Add mushrooms to the fried onions.

Step 4 Add meat, olives and seasoning to sauce.

Cook's Notes

 Time
Preparation takes 10 minutes, cooking takes 15 minutes.

 **Cook's Tip**
When slicing the meat ensure you cut across the grain as this helps to cook the meat quickly.

Watchpoint
Always ensure the pasta is well drained otherwise it will spoil the consistency of the sauce.

SERVES 4

SPAGHETTI MARINARA

This delightful recipe is perfect for special occasions or as a weekend treat.

45g/1½oz can anchovy fillets
75ml/5 tbsps water
75ml/5 tbsps dry white wine
1 bay leaf
4 peppercorns
225g/8oz scallops, cleaned and sliced
2 tbsps olive oil
2 cloves garlic, crushed
1 tsp basil
400g/14oz can plum tomatoes, seeded and chopped
1 tbsp tomato purée
300g/10oz spaghetti
450g/1lb cooked prawns, shelled and de-veined
2 tbsps chopped parsley
Salt and pepper

Step 4 Add tomatoes, anchovies and tomato purée.

Step 6 Add seafood to sauce.

Step 2 Add scallops to pan, cook for 2 minutes then drain.

1. Drain anchovies and cut into small pieces. Set aside.

2. Place water, wine, bay leaf and peppercorns in a pan. Heat to a slow boil. Add scallops and cook for 2 minutes. Remove and drain.

3. Heat the oil, add garlic and basil, and cook for 30 seconds.

4. Add tomatoes, anchovies and tomato purée to the garlic. Stir until combined. Cook for 10 minutes.

5. Meanwhile, cook the spaghetti in a large pan of boiling, salted water for 10 minutes, or until tender, but still firm. Drain.

6. Add seafood to sauce, and cook a further 1 minute. Add 1 tbsp parsley and stir through. Season with salt and pepper to taste. Toss gently.

7. Pour sauce over spaghetti and serve immediately, sprinkled with remaining parsley.

Cook's Notes

Time
Preparation takes 10 minutes, cooking takes 20 minutes.

Variation
Replace some, or all, of the prawns and scallops with the fresh seafood cocktails now available in many supermarkets.

Buying Guide
When buying seafood try your local fishmonger as it is often better value than the supermarket.

SERVES 4

MACARONI CHEESE WITH ANCHOVIES

Macaroni cheese is given a new twist with the addition of anchovies.

60g/2oz can anchovy fillets
225g/8oz macaroni
60g/2oz butter or margarine
60g/2oz flour
570ml/1 pint milk
½ tsp dry mustard
175g/6oz Gruyère or Cheddar cheese, grated
Salt
Pepper

turn to heat and bring to the boil. Simmer for 3 minutes, stirring continuously.

5. Stir in the mustard, anchovies, and half the cheese. Season with salt and pepper to taste. Stir in the macaroni, and pour into an oven-proof dish.

6. Sprinkle the remaining cheese over the top, and make a lattice work with the remaining anchovies. Brown under a hot grill. Serve immediately.

Step 3 Melt butter, stir in flour and gradually add milk.

Step 5 Add anchovies, mustard and half of the cheese.

Step 6 Arrange reserved anchovies to form a lattice pattern.

1. Drain anchovies, and set enough aside to slice to make a thin lattice over the dish. Chop the rest finely.

2. Cook the macaroni in plenty of boiling, salted water for 10 minutes, or until tender but still firm. Rinse in hot water and drain well.

3. Meanwhile, melt the butter in a pan. Stir in the flour and cook for 1 minute.

4. Remove from heat, and gradually stir in the milk. Re-

Cook's Notes

Time
Preparation takes 5 minutes, cooking takes 15 minutes.

Serving Idea
Serve this hearty dish with crusty bread and a green salad.

Variation
Try using wholemeal macaroni for a change of flavour.

SERVES 4-6

PENNE WITH SPICY CHILLI SAUCE

Penne are hollow pasta tubes which can be bought at
most supermarkets. Macaroni can be used equally
as well.

450g/1lb canned plum tomatoes
1 tbsp olive oil
2 cloves garlic, crushed
1 onion, chopped
4 rashers of bacon, chopped
2 red chilli peppers, seeded and chopped
2 spring onions, chopped
60g/2oz pecorino or Parmesan cheese, grated
450g/1lb penne or macaroni
Salt and pepper

1. Chop the tomatoes and sieve them to remove the pips.

2. Heat the oil in a frying pan and fry the garlic, onion and bacon gently for 6-8 minutes.

3. Add the sieved tomatoes, the chilli peppers, chopped spring onions and half of the cheese. Simmer gently for 20 minutes. Season to taste.

4. Cook the penne or macaroni in boiling water for 10-15 minutes, or until tender. Rinse under hot water and drain well.

5. Put the cooked penne into a warm serving dish and toss them in half of the sauce. Pour the remaining sauce over the top and sprinkle with the remaining cheese.

Step 3 Stir the sieved tomatoes, chilli peppers, spring onions and half the cheese into the onion mixture.

Step 5 Toss the cooked penne in half of the sauce, mixing together well to coat evenly.

Cook's Notes

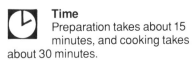
Time
Preparation takes about 15 minutes, and cooking takes about 30 minutes.

Variation
Substitute 60g/2oz chopped button mushrooms for the bacon.

Serving Ideas
Garnish the serving dish with spring onion flowers and serve with a mixed green salad.

SERVES 6

SPAGHETTI WITH CRAB AND BACON

This recipe includes a wonderful preparation of home-made parsley pasta. It is served with crab and bacon, and tossed in a seafood sauce.

1 bunch flat-leaved parsley (approximately 6 tbsps)
500g/1lb 2oz flour
4 eggs
225g/8oz bacon
1 tbsp olive oil
10 (12oz) crab sticks
375ml/13 fl oz double cream
3 tbsps butter
Fresh chervil
Salt and pepper

1. Trim the leaves off the parsley. Cook for 10 minutes in boiling water. Pass through a fine sieve and reserve the cooking liquid. Purée the parsley with 3 tbsps of the cooking liquid in a blender.

2. In a bowl, mix together the flour, salt, eggs and 1½ tbsps parsley purée. Form into a ball.

3. Quarter the dough and form these pieces into balls. Press each ball flat and run it through a pasta machine.

4. Thin the dough progressively by passing it through the machine several times. Flour the dough frequently throughout the operation. Run the flattened strips of dough through the spaghetti cutter.

5. Cut the rind off the bacon and cut the bacon first into strips and then into small rectangles.

6. Add the olive oil to boiling, salted water and cook the spaghetti for 5 minutes. Strain and rinse.

7. Shred the crab sticks with your fingers.

Step 7 Shred crab sticks with your fingers.

Step 8 Add bacon and crab to heated cream.

8. Heat the cream gently with the crab and bacon pieces.

9. Meanwhile, heat the butter in a pan and when it bubbles, add the spaghetti (first reheated by plunging for 30 seconds in boiling water). Mix well and season with salt and pepper.

10. Place the buttered spaghetti around the edges of the dinner plates and arrange the crab/bacon mixture in the centre. Garnish with chopped fresh chervil.

Cook's Notes

Time
Preparation takes 1 hour, cooking takes 20 minutes.

Variation
Use fresh crab meat instead of crab sticks.

Cook's Tip
Be careful not to overheat the cream or it will curdle.

SERVES 6

TAGLIATELLE WITH BLUE CHEESE

Freshly-made pasta noodles are tossed with a creamy sauce flavoured with blue cheese and diced, dried apricots.

500g/1lb 2oz flour mixed with a pinch of salt
5 eggs
1 tbsp olive oil
120g/4oz blue cheese (Roquefort, Stilton)
150g/5oz dried apricots
300ml/10 fl oz double cream
60ml/2 fl oz milk
2 egg yolks
30g/1oz pine nuts
½ bunch chives
Salt and pepper

1. In a bowl, work together the flour and eggs, to form a soft ball of dough.

2. Quarter the dough and flatten each piece. Dredge each piece with plenty of flour. Flour the rollers of a pasta machine, and either pass the dough through the machine or roll it out.

3. Continue rolling the pasta until thin. Flour frequently during the process. Thread the dough strips through the tagliatelle cutter, or cut into strips with a knife. Dredge the tagliatelle with flour and allow to dry for 2 hours.

4. Bring a saucepan of salted water to a boil with 1 tbsp oil. Cook the pasta for 2 to 4 minutes, stirring with a fork. Drain the tagliatelle and rinse in plenty of cold water to prevent sticking. Set aside.

5. Break up the cheese and force through a sieve with the back of a spoon.

6. Cut the apricot into strips, then dice.

7. Slowly heat the cream in a saucepan. Stir in the cheese and milk. Blend until smooth with a hand-held electric blender.

8. Whilst the sauce is hot, stir in the tagliatelle, and apricots, and season again, as necessary. Heat through quickly, so the cream does not curdle nor the noodles overcook.

9. Mix the pasta with two forks. Remove from the heat, and mix in the egg yolks and the pine nuts.

10. Chop the chives finely and sprinkle them over the tagliatelle; serve immediately.

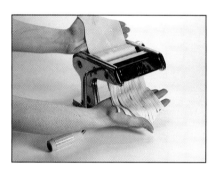

Step 3 Thread dough through tagliatelle cutter.

Step 6 Cut the apricots into strips then dice.

Cook's Notes

Time
Preparation takes 1 hour plus 2 hours to dry the pasta. Cooking takes 15 minutes.

Variation
Substitute your favourite dried fruit for the apricots.

Cook's Tip
Don't worry if you don't have a pasta machine, it simply means you have to roll out the pasta by hand, and the tagliatelle strips will be a little less straight!

SERVES 4

MEAT RAVIOLI

Don't be put off by the number of ingredients in this recipe,
it's delicious and well worth the effort.

Filling
60g/2oz butter or margarine
1 clove garlic, crushed
1 onion, peeled and grated
225g/8oz minced beef
75ml/5 tbsps red wine
Salt
Pepper
2 tbsps breadcrumbs
120g/4oz cooked spinach, chopped
2 eggs, beaten

Dough
275g/9oz strong plain flour
Pinch of salt
3 eggs

Sauce
400g/14oz can plum tomatoes
1 small onion, peeled and grated
1 small carrot, diced finely
1 bay leaf
3 parsley stalks
Salt
Pepper
60g/2oz Parmesan cheese, grated

1. To make the filling, heat butter in pan. Add garlic and onion, and fry gently for 1 minute. Add minced beef, and fry until browned. Add red wine, and salt and pepper to taste, and cook, uncovered, for 15 minutes.

2. Strain juices and reserve them for sauce. Allow mixture to cool. Add breadcrumbs, chopped spinach, and beaten eggs to bind. Adjust salt and pepper to taste.

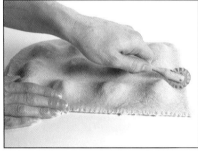

Step 5 Place the balls of filling on the dough about 4cm/1½ inches apart. Cut with a ravioli cutter or a pastry wheel.

3. To make dough, sift flour in a bowl with the salt. Make a well in the centre and add the eggs. Work flour and eggs together with a spoon, then knead by hand, until a smooth dough is formed. Leave dough to rest for 15 minutes.

4. Lightly flour a board, and roll out dough thinly into a rectangle. Cut dough in half.

5. Shape the filling into small balls, and set them about 4cm/1½ inches apart on one half of the dough.

6. Place the other half on top and cut with a ravioli cutter or small pastry cutter. Seal the edges by pinching together.

7. Cook in batches in a large, wide pan with plenty of boiling, salted water until tender – about 8 minutes. Remove carefully with a perforated spoon.

8. To make the sauce, put all ingredients in a saucepan. Add juice from cooked meat, and bring to the boil. Simmer for 10 minutes.

9. Push sauce through a sieve, and return smooth mixture to pan. Adjust seasoning.

10. Put ravioli in a warm dish and cover with tomato sauce. Serve immediately, with grated Parmesan cheese.

Cook's Notes

Time
Preparation takes 30 minutes, cooking takes 30 minutes.

Cook's Tip
Always buy fresh Parmesan and grate it yourself rather than buying the pre-packaged variety.

Watchpoint
Ensure the spinach is well drained before adding to the filling.

SERVES 4

TORTELLINI

Tortellini tastes wonderful and it is well worth the effort to
make your own.

Filling
30g/1oz cream cheese
1 cooked chicken breast, finely diced
30g/1oz ham, finely diced
2 spinach leaves, stalks removed, cooked and
   chopped finely
1 tbsp grated Parmesan cheese
1 egg, beaten
Salt
Pepper

Dough
300g/10oz strong plain flour
Pinch of salt
1 tbsp water
1 tbsp oil
3 eggs

Sauce
280ml/½ pint single cream
60g/2oz mushrooms, cleaned and sliced
60g/2oz Parmesan cheese, grated
1 tbsp chopped parsley
Salt
Pepper

1. To make the filling, beat the cream cheese until soft and smooth. Add chicken, ham, spinach and Parmesan cheese, and mix well.

2. Add egg gradually, and salt and pepper to taste. Set aside.

3. To make the dough, sift flour and salt onto a board.

Make a well in the centre. Mix water, oil and lightly-beaten egg together, and gradually pour into well, working in the flour with the other hand, a little at a time.

4. Continue until the mixture comes together in a firm ball of dough. Knead on a lightly-floured board for 5 minutes, or until smooth and elastic. Put into a bowl, cover with a cloth, and set aside for 15 minutes.

5. Roll dough out on a lightly-floured board as thinly as possible. Using a 5cm/2 inch cutter, cut out rounds.

6. Put ½ teaspoon of filling into the centre of each round. Fold in half, pressing edges together firmly. Wrap around forefinger, and press ends together.

Step 6 Place ½ teaspoon filling onto each round of dough. Wrap tortellini around forefinger and press ends together.

7. Cook in batches in a large pan, in plenty of boiling salted water for about 10 minutes until tender, stirring occasionally.

8. To make the sauce, meanwhile, gently heat cream in a pan. Add mushrooms, Parmesan cheese, parsley, and salt and pepper to taste. Gently cook for 3 minutes.

9. Toss sauce together with tortellini. Serve immediately, sprinkled with parsley.

Cook's Notes

Time
Preparation takes 30 minutes, cooking takes 15 minutes.

Cook's Tip
Add a tablespoon of olive oil when boiling the pasta as this stops it sticking.

SERVES 4

ITALIAN CASSEROLE

Salami, cheese, macaroni, peppers and olives – combine
them and you have the perfect family meal.

90g/3oz small macaroni
60g/2oz butter or margarine
1 onion, peeled and chopped
1 clove garlic, crushed
2 × 400g/14oz can plum tomatoes
1 tbsp tomato purée
1 red pepper, cored, seeds removed, and chopped
    roughly
1 green pepper, cored, seeds removed, and chopped
    roughly
225g/8oz salami, cut into chunks
10 black olives, halved, and stones removed
Salt
Pepper
120g/4oz Mozzarella cheese, sliced thinly

1. Cook the macaroni in plenty of boiling, salted water for
10 minutes, or until tender but still firm.

2. Rinse under hot water and drain well. Place in a shallow, oven-proof dish.

3. Meanwhile, heat butter in pan, and fry onion and garlic
gently until soft.

4. Add undrained tomatoes, tomato purée, red and
green peppers, salami and olives, and stir well. Simmer,
uncovered, for 5 minutes. Season with salt and pepper.

5. Pour over the macaroni, stir, and cover with the sliced
cheese.

6. Bake uncovered in a moderate oven at 180°C/350°F/
Gas Mark 4 for 20 minutes, until cheese has melted. Serve immediately.

Step 2 Place drained macaroni in the base of a shallow ovenproof dish.

Step 4 Add peppers to other ingredients in pan.

Step 5 Cover macaroni with slices of cheese.

Cook's Notes

Time
Preparation takes 15 minutes,
cooking takes 40 minutes.

Variation
Vary the amount of garlic in
this dish according to taste.

Serving Idea
This is a hearty dish and only
needs a green salad and
bread to accompany it.

SERVES 4
FISH RAVIOLI

Ravioli stuffed with fish is a little unusual, but it tastes
absolutely wonderful.

Filling
225g/8oz sole fillets, or other flat fish, skinned and
  boned
1 slice of onion
1 slice of lemon
6 peppercorns
1 bay leaf
1 tbsp lemon juice
280ml/½ pint water
2 eggs, beaten
2 tbsps breadcrumbs
1 spring onion, finely chopped

Dough
275g/9oz strong plain flour
Pinch of salt
3 eggs

Lemon sauce
30g/1oz butter or margarine
30g/1oz flour
280ml/½ pint strained cooking liquid from fish
2 tbsps double cream
Salt
Pepper
2 tbsps lemon juice

1. Pre-heat oven to 180°C/350°F/Gas Mark 4.

2. Wash and dry fish. Place in oven-proof dish with slice
of onion, slice of lemon, peppercorns, bay leaf, lemon
juice and water. Cover and cook in oven for 20 minutes.

3. Remove fish from liquid and allow to drain. Strain
liquid, and set aside. When fish is cool, beat with the back
of a spoon to a pulp.

4 Add eggs, breadcrumbs and spring onions, and salt

and pepper to taste. Mix well.

5. Sift flour into a bowl and add the salt. Make a well in
the centre, and add the eggs. Work the flour and eggs
together with a spoon, and then knead by hand, until a
smooth dough is formed. Leave to rest for 15 minutes.

6. Lightly flour a board, and roll out dough thinly into a
rectangle. Cut dough in half. Shape the filling into small
balls, and set them about 4cm/1½ inches apart on one
half of the dough. Place the other half on top, and cut with
a ravioli cutter or small pastry cutter. Seal the edges.

Step 6 Shape filling into small balls and place on the dough.

7. Cook in batches in a large, wide pan with plenty of boiling, salted water until tender – about 8 minutes. Remove
carefully with a perforated spoon. Meanwhile, make
sauce.

8. Melt butter in pan. Stir in flour, and cook for 30 seconds. Draw off heat and gradually stir in liquid from
cooked fish.

9. Return to heat and bring to the boil. Simmer for 4
minutes, stirring continuously. Add cream and mix well.
Season to taste.

10. Remove from heat, and gradually stir in lemon juice.
Do not reboil.

11. Pour sauce over ravioli and serve immediately.

Cook's Notes

 Time
Preparation takes 30 minutes,
cooking takes 30 minutes.

Buying Guide
Use whatever flat fish is
currently best value.

 Watchpoint
Stir the white sauce
thoroughly when adding the
milk or it will form lumps.

SERVES 4

TAGLIATELLE WITH CREAMY LIVER SAUCE

Chicken livers are married with cream and mushrooms in this unusual dish.

2 medium onions, peeled and sliced
1 clove garlic, crushed
60ml/4 tbsps olive oil
120g/4oz mushrooms, sliced
450g/1lb chicken livers, cleaned and sliced
120ml/8 tbsps single cream
2 eggs, beaten
Salt and pepper
300g/10oz tagliatelle
1 tbsp chopped parsley

1. In a large frying pan, cook onions and garlic gently in oil until softened.

2. Add mushrooms and cook for 3 minutes. Add chicken livers to onions and mushrooms, and cook until lightly browned.

3. Remove from heat and stir in cream. Return to low heat and cook, uncovered, for further 2 minutes.

4. Remove from heat, and stir in lightly beaten eggs. Season with salt and pepper to taste.

5. Meanwhile, cook the tagliatelle in plenty of boiling, salted water for 10 minutes, or until tender but still firm, stirring occasionally.

6. Drain tagliatelle, toss in olive oil and black pepper. Serve sauce over tagliatelle and sprinkle with parsley.

Step 4 Remove pan from heat and stir in beaten eggs.

Step 2 Add chicken livers to pan.

Step 6 Spoon sauce over the tagliatelle to serve.

Cook's Notes

Time
Preparation takes 10 minutes, cooking takes 15 minutes.

Watchpoint
Be careful not to over-cook the livers as they will toughen.

SERVES 4

SPINACH LASAGNE

This is a great family favourite and no wonder, it is filling,
tasty and economical.

8 sheets green lasagne pasta

Spinach sauce
60g/4 tbsps butter or margarine
325g/11oz packet of frozen spinach, thawed and
    chopped finely
Pinch of ground nutmeg
60g/4 tbsps flour
280ml/½ pint milk
Salt
Pepper

Mornay sauce
30g/1oz butter or margarine
30g/1oz flour
280ml/½ pint milk
90g/3oz Parmesan cheese, grated
1 tsp French mustard
Salt

1. To make the spinach sauce, heat butter in pan, stir in flour and cook for 30 seconds. Draw off heat, and stir in milk gradually.

2. Return to heat, and bring to the boil, stirring continuously. Cook for 3 minutes.

3. Add spinach, nutmeg, and salt and pepper to taste. Set aside.

4. Cook spinach lasagne in lots of boiling, salted water for 10 minutes, or until tender. Rinse in cold water, and drain carefully. Dry on a clean cloth.

5. To make mornay sauce, heat butter in pan and stir in flour, cooking for 30 seconds. Remove from heat, and stir in milk. Return to heat, stirring continuously, until boiling.

6. Continue stirring, and simmer for 3 minutes. Draw off heat, and add mustard, two-thirds of cheese, and salt to taste.

7. Grease an oven-proof baking dish. Line the base with a layer of lasagne, followed by some of the spinach mixture, and a layer of cheese sauce. Repeat the process, finishing with a layer of lasagne and a covering of cheese sauce.

8. Sprinkle with the remaining cheese. Bake in a hot oven at 200°C/400°F/Gas Mark 6 until golden on top. Serve immediately.

Step 6 Add the mustard and ⅔ of the cheese.

Step 7 Line the base of a greased dish with lasagne, the spinach mixture and cheese sauce, then repeat.

Cook's Notes

Time
Preparation takes 10 minutes, cooking takes 30 minutes.

Cook's Tip
Add a tablespoon of olive oil to the boiling water when cooking the lasagne to prevent it sticking together.

Watchpoint
If the top of the lasagne does not brown sufficiently, finish it off under the grill.

SERVES 4

PASTITSIO

A hearty mixture of macaroni and minced beef make this
the perfect winter meal.

225g/8oz macaroni
90g/3oz butter or margarine
60g/2oz Parmesan cheese, grated
Pinch of grated nutmeg
Salt
Pepper
2 eggs, beaten
1 medium onion, peeled and chopped
1 clove garlic, crushed
450g/1lb minced beef
2 tbsps tomato purée
90ml/6 tbsps beef stock
2 tbsps chopped parsley
60ml/4 tbsps red wine
30g/1oz plain flour
280ml/½ pint milk

Step 3 Add half
the cheese and
the nutmeg to the
pasta.

Step 8 Spoon
second layer of
macaroni over
mince.

1. Preheat oven to 190°C/375°F/Gas Mark 5.

2. Cook macaroni in plenty of boiling salted water for 10
minutes, or until tender but still firm. Rinse under hot
water. Drain.

3. Put one-third of the butter in the pan and return macaroni to it. Add half the cheese, nutmeg, and salt and
pepper to taste. Leave to cool.

4. Mix in half the beaten egg, and put aside.

5. Melt half of the remaining butter in a pan, and fry onion
and garlic gently until onion is soft. Increase temperature,
add meat, and fry until browned.

6. Add tomato purée, stock, parsley and wine, and season with salt and pepper.

7. Simmer for 20 minutes. In a small pan, melt the rest of
the butter. Stir in the flour and cook for 30 seconds. Remove from heat, and stir in milk. Bring to boil, stirring continuously, until the sauce thickens. Beat in the remaining
egg and season to taste.

8. Spoon half the macaroni into a serving-dish and cover
with the meat sauce. Put on another layer of macaroni
and smooth over.

9. Pour over white sauce, sprinkle with remaining
cheese, and bake in the oven for 30 minutes until golden
brown. Serve immediately.

Cook's Notes

Time
Preparation takes 10 minutes,
cooking takes 1 hour.

Serving Idea
Serve with green vegetables
and crusty bread.

Cook's Tip
Finish the dish off under the
grill for a lovely golden top.

SERVES 4

SALMON AND FENNEL LASAGNE

Thin strips of pasta are pre-cooked and then layered with salmon and white sauce. Absolutely mouthwatering!

350g/12oz flour, sifted
3 eggs, beaten
225ml/8 fl oz fairly runny béchamel sauce
600g/1⅓lbs salmon (in one long strip if possible)
1 tsp fennel seeds
4 tbsps grated cheese
225ml/8 fl oz fish stock
30g/1oz butter
Salt and pepper

Step 3 Cut the salmon into thin slices.

1. Make the dough by mixing together the flour, a good pinch of salt and the 3 eggs. Set the dough aside to rest for 30 minutes and then roll out very thinly into long strips.

2. Part-cook the pasta in salted, boiling water for 1 minute. Drain and then lay out on damp tea towels, without overlapping the strips.

3. Cut the salmon into thin slices – a very sharp knife with a finely serrated blade is best for this delicate job. Remove all the bones.

4. Butter an ovenproof dish and place strips of pasta into the base.

5. Now build up layers of white sauce, a few fennel seeds, the salmon, salt, pepper and then another layer of pasta. Continue layering these ingredients until they are all used up, finishing with a layer of pasta.

6. Pour over the fish stock and then sprinkle over the cheese. Cook in a hot oven at 200°C/400°F/Gas Mark 6 for about 15-20 minutes, or until the fish stock has been almost completely absorbed.

Step 5 Pour layer of sauce over the pasta.

Step 5 Arrange salmon over the sauce.

Cook's Notes

Time
Preparation takes about 40 minutes and cooking takes approximately 35 minutes.

Serving Idea
This lasagne can be served with a cream sauce made by gently heating a little cream with 1 tsp fennel seeds.

Cook's Tip
This lasagne should be slightly crisp and golden on top. If necessary, place the dish under a hot grill for 1 minute.

SERVES 4

MACARONI CHEESE WITH FRANKFURTERS

A hearty family supper dish, ideal for cold winter evenings.

8 frankfurter sausages
450g/1lb macaroni
60g/2oz butter or margarine
60g/2oz plain flour
570ml/1 pint milk
180g/6oz Cheddar cheese, grated
1 tsp dry mustard powder
Salt and pepper

1. Poach the frankfurters for 5-6 minutes in slightly salted boiling water.

2. Remove the skins from the frankfurters if preferred and, when cold, slice the meat diagonally.

3. Cook the macaroni in plenty of boiling, salted water for about 20 minutes, or until tender.

4. Rinse in cold water and drain well.

5. Melt the butter in a saucepan. Stir in the flour and cook for 1 minute.

6. Remove the pan from the heat and add the milk gradually, beating thoroughly and returning the pan to the heat to cook between additions. When all the milk has been added, simmer for 2 minutes, stirring occasionally.

7. Stir the frankfurters, grated cheese and mustard into the sauce mixture. Season to taste.

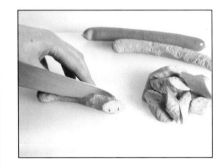

Step 2 Remove the skins from the frankfurters and when they are completely cold, cut them diagonally into slices about 2.5cm/1 inch long.

Step 6 Add the milk gradually to the melted butter and flour mixture, reheating and beating the mixture well between additions, until all the milk is incorporated and the sauce is thick and smooth.

Cook's Notes

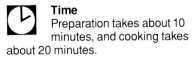 **Time**
Preparation takes about 10 minutes, and cooking takes about 20 minutes.

Variation
Use 180g/6oz of chopped, grilled or fried bacon instead of the frankfurters.

 Serving Ideas
To serve, make a lattice of pepper strips over the top of the dish before grilling, and serve with a mixed salad.

SERVES 6-8

LAMB WITH PASTA AND TOMATOES

Lamb appears in many different guises in Greek cuisine;
this recipe offers a delicious blend of subtle tastes.

1 leg or shoulder of lamb
2 cloves garlic, peeled and cut into thin slivers
60ml/4 tbsps olive oil
50g/1lb fresh tomatoes or 400g/14oz canned tomatoes
15ml/1 tbsp chopped fresh oregano
Salt and pepper
570ml/1 pint lamb or beef stock or water
225g/8oz pasta shells, spirals or other shapes
Finely grated Parmesan cheese

1. Cut slits at about 5cm/2 inch intervals all over the lamb. Insert small slivers of garlic into each slit. Place the lamb in a large baking dish and rub the surface with the olive oil.

2. Cook in a preheated oven at 220°C/425°F/Gas Mark 7 for about 50 minutes, basting occasionally.

3. Meanwhile, parboil the pasta for about 5 minutes and rinse in hot water to remove the starch.

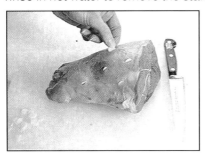

Step 1 Cut slits at intervals all over the lamb with a small, sharp knife. Insert slivers of garlic into each cut.

Step 4 Mix the tomatoes with oregano, salt and pepper and pour over the lamb.

Step 4 Once the pasta is added to the lamb, take the dish out of the oven occasionally and stir so that the pasta cooks evenly.

4. Turn the meat over and add the stock or water, pasta and additional seasoning. Mix the tomatoes with the oregano, salt and pepper and pour over the lamb. Stir well. Cook an additional 20-30 minutes, stirring the pasta occasionally to ensure even cooking.

5. When the pasta is completely cooked, turn the lamb over again and sprinkle with cheese to serve. Serve directly from the dish or transfer to a large, deep serving place.

Cook's Notes

Cook's Tip
If the meat reaches desired doneness before the pasta is cooked, remove it to a serving plate and keep it warm. Continue cooking the pasta, covering the dish to speed things up.

Variation
The dish can be made without tomatoes, if desired. Beef can be sustituted for the lamb and the cooking time increased.

Time
Preparation takes about 20 minutes, cooking takes about 1 hour 35 minutes.

SERVES 4

MEAT RAVIOLI WITH RED PEPPER SAUCE

Pepper-flavoured pasta dough is rolled thinly, cut into squares, filled with a delicious meat stuffing and served with a creamy red pepper sauce.

2 red peppers, seeded
200g/7oz flour, sifted
2 eggs
200g/7oz minced beef
1 tbsp finely chopped parsley
½ onion, chopped
120ml/4 fl oz single cream
90g/3oz butter
salt and pepper

1. Place the red peppers in a food processor and blend until liquid. Place in a small bowl and set aside, giving time for the pulp to rise to the surface. This takes approximately 30 minutes.

2. To make the dough, place the sifted flour in a bowl with a pinch of salt. Add 1 egg and 45ml/3 tbsps of the pulp (not the juice).

3. Mix together really well and form into a ball. Set the dough aside for 30 minutes.

4. Mix together the meat, parsley and onion, and season with salt and pepper.

5. Roll the dough out very thinly, using a pasta machine if available, and cut into small squares. Place a little stuffing on half of the cut squares.

6. Beat the remaining egg and brush the edges of the squares with the egg. Cover with another square of dough and seal the edges by pinching together with your fingers.

7. Bring a large saucepan of salted water to the boil and cook the ravioli for approximately 3 minutes – longer if you prefer your pasta well cooked.

8. While the ravioli are cooking, prepare the sauce by heating the cream with 100ml/4 fl oz of the red pepper pulp. Bring to the boil and then whisk in the butter.

9. Drain the ravioli and then pat them dry with a tea towel. Serve with the hot cream sauce.

Step 5 Cut pasta into small squares.

Step 6 Brush edges with beaten egg.

Cook's Notes

Time
Preparation takes about 50 minutes, resting time 30 minutes and cooking time approximately 15 minutes.

Variation
Add a little wine vinegar (1 tsp) and a few drops of Tabasco to the sauce to give it a slightly peppery taste.

Watchpoint
When rolling out the dough, flour it well so that it does not stick to the rolling pin or pasta machine rollers.

SERVES 4-6

PORK & PRAWN CHOW MEIN

Chinese chow mein dishes are usually based on noodles,
using more expensive ingredients in small amounts. This
makes economical everyday fare.

225g/8oz medium dried Chinese noodles
225g/8oz pork fillet, thinly sliced
1 carrot, peeled and shredded
1 small red pepper, cored, seeded and thinly sliced
90g/3oz bean sprouts
60g/2oz mange tout
15ml/1 tbsp rice wine or dry sherry
30ml/2 tbsps soy sauce
120g/4oz peeled, cooked prawns

Step 3 Cut peppers in half and remove the cores and seeds. Make sure all the white pith is also removed before slicing thinly.

Step 1 Place whole sheets of noodles into rapidly boiling salted water. Stir as the noodles start to soften.

Step 4 Add the cooked noodles to the other ingredients in the wok and use chopsticks to toss over high heat.

1. Cook the noodles in plenty of boiling salted water for about 4-5 minutes. Rinse under hot water and drain thoroughly.

2. Heat the wok and add oil. Stir-fry the pork 4-5 minutes or until almost cooked. Add the carrots to the wok and cook for 1-2 minutes.

3. Core, seed and slice the red pepper and add the remaining vegetables, wine and soy sauce. Cook for about 2 minutes.

4. Add the cooked, drained noodles and prawns and toss over heat for 1-2 minutes. Serve immediately.

Cook's Notes

Time
Preparation takes about 20 minutes. The noodles take 4-5 minutes to cook and the stir-fried ingredients need to cook for about 5-6 minutes for the pork and about 3 minutes for the vegetables.

Variation
Use green pepper instead of red, or add other vegetables such as baby corn ears, mushrooms or peas.

Buying Guide
Dried Chinese noodles are available in three thicknesses. Thin noodles are usually reserved for soup, while medium and thick noodles are used for fried dishes.

Chapter 5

Desserts

SERVES 4

BLACK CHERRY RAVIOLI WITH SOURED CREAM SAUCE

Black cherries and pasta are a wonderful contrast to the cream in this lovely dessert.

Dough
275g/9oz strong plain flour
1 tbsp sugar
3 eggs

Large can black cherries, pips removed
60g/2oz granulated sugar
1 tsp arrowroot
120ml/4 fl oz soured cream
120ml/4 fl oz double cream

Step 3 Roll the dough out into a thin rectangle.

1. Put cherries in a sieve. Strain off juice and reserve.

2. Make dough by sifting flour and sugar in a bowl. Make a well in the centre and add the lightly-beaten eggs. Work flour and eggs together with a spoon, and then by hand, until a smooth dough is formed. Knead gently.

3. Lightly flour board, and roll dough out thinly into a rectangle. Cut dough in half.

4. Put well-drained cherries about 4cm/1½ inches apart on the dough. Place the other half on top, and cut with a small glass or pastry cutter. Seal well around edges with the back of a fork.

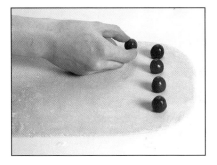

Step 4 Place the well-drained cherries about 4cm/1½ inches apart on the dough.

5. Boil plenty of water in a large saucepan, and drop in cherry pasta. Cook for about 10 minutes, or until they rise to the surface. Remove with a draining spoon and keep warm.

6. Keep 2 tablespoons cherry juice aside. Mix 1 tablespoon cherry juice with arrowroot. Mix remaining juice with sugar and set over heat. Add arrowroot mixture, and heat until it thickens.

Step 4 Cut the pasta with a pastry cutter.

7. Meanwhile mix soured cream and double cream together and marble 1 tablespoon of cherry juice through it.

8. Pour hot, thickened cherry juice over cherry ravioli. Serve hot with cream sauce.

Cook's Notes

Time
Preparation takes 30 minutes, cooking takes 15 minutes.

Variation
Cut the ravioli into different shapes such as stars, but ensure they are well sealed around the edges.

Cook's Tip
If you want to reduce the amount of calories in this recipe, replace the cream with yogurt.

SERVES 4

HONEY VERMICELLI

Honey, sesame seeds and cinnamon combine beautifully
with pasta and cream in this unusual dessert.

225g/8oz vermicelli
60g/2oz butter
2 tsps sesame seeds
3 tbsps clear honey
¼ tsp cinnamon

Sauce
75ml/5 tbsps double cream
75ml/5 tbsps soured cream

Step 4 Melt the butter and fry sesame seeds.

Step 2 Spread drained vermicelli out to dry on a wire tray covered with paper towels.

Step 5 Add vermicelli and heat through.

1. Cook vermicelli in boiling, salted water for 5 minutes or until tender, stirring regularly with a fork to separate noodles.

2. Drain, and spread out to dry on a wire tray covered with absorbent paper, or a tea-towel. Leave for about an hour.

3. Make the sauce by mixing the soured cream and double cream together.

4. Melt the butter in frying pan. Add sesame seeds, and fry until lightly golden.

5. Stir in honey, cinnamon and vermicelli, and heat through. Serve hot, topped with the cream sauce.

Cook's Notes

Time
Preparation takes 1 hour, cooking takes 15 minutes.

Variation
For a healthier option, serve the vermicelli topped with natural yogurt or fromage frais.

Buying Guide
If your supermarket stocks both dried and fresh pasta, buy the fresh variety as it tastes better.

SERVES 4

CHOCOLATE CREAM HELÈNE

A simple dessert which is nonetheless delicious.

90g/3oz soup pasta
450ml/¾ pint milk
45g/1½oz caster sugar
1 tsp cocoa
1 tbsp hot water
140ml/¼ pint cream, lightly whipped
1 large can pear halves

Garnish
Chocolate, grated

1. Cook pasta in milk and sugar until soft. Stir regularly, being careful not to allow it to boil over.

2. Meanwhile, dissolve cocoa in hot water, and stir into pasta.

Step 2 Dissolve cocoa in hot water and stir into the pasta.

3. Pour pasta into a bowl to cool. When cool, fold in lightly-whipped cream. Chill.

4. Serve with pear halves, and a sprinkling of grated chocolate.

Step 3 Fold in the lightly whipped cream.

Step 4 Serve with pear halves and a sprinkling of grated chocolate.

Cook's Notes

 Time
Preparation takes 15 minutes, cooking takes 10 minutes.

 Variation
Use other soft fruits such as strawberries instead of the pears.

SERVES 4

CREAM CHEESE MARGHERITA

This unusual mixture of ingredients has wonderful texture
and flavour.

60g/2oz sultanas
Juice and grated rind of ½ a lemon
120g/4oz soup pasta
225g/8oz packet cream cheese
60g/2oz caster sugar
140ml/¼ pint single cream
½ tsp ground cinnamon

Garnish
1 tbsp flaked almonds
Lemon peel, cut into slivers

Step 3 Work the cream cheese, sugar and cream together.

1. Soak sultanas in lemon juice for about 1 hour.

2. Meanwhile, cook the pasta in plenty of boiling, lightly-salted water until tender, stirring occasionally.

3. Work the cream cheese, sugar and cream together

until smooth.

4. Beat in grated lemon rind and cinnamon.

5. Fold in pasta and sultanas.

6. Divide between individual dessert glasses or small sweet dishes, and cover top with flaked almond and slivers of lemon peel. Chill before serving.

Step 4 Beat in the grated lemon rind and cinnamon.

Step 5 Fold in the pasta and sultanas.

Cook's Notes

Time
Preparation takes 1 hour, cooking takes 10 minutes.

Variation
Substitute different dried fruits, such as apricots, for the sultanas.

SERVES 4

VANILLA CREAM MELBA

Pasta is wonderful in desserts as it soaks up flavours
beautifully.

90g/3oz soup pasta
450ml/¾ pint milk
45g/1½oz brown sugar
Few drops vanilla essence
140ml/¼ pint cream, lightly whipped
1 can peach halves
1 tsp cinnamon (optional)

Melba sauce
225g/8oz raspberries
30g/1oz icing sugar

Step 4 Push the
raspberries
through a sieve.

Step 5 Serve
pasta with peach
halves.

Step 3 Fold
cream into cooled
pasta mixture.

1. Cook pasta in milk and sugar until soft. Stir regularly, being careful not to allow it to boil over.

2. Draw off heat and stir in vanilla essence.

3. Pour pasta into a bowl to cool. When cool, fold in

cream. Chill.

4. Meanwhile, make Melba sauce. Push raspberries through a sieve. Mix in icing sugar to desired thickness and taste.

5. Serve pasta with peach halves and Melba sauce. Dust with cinnamon if desired.

Cook's Notes

Time
Preparation takes 15 minutes,
cooking takes 10 minutes.

Cook's Tip
Use fresh peaches when they
are in season as they taste far
superior to the tinned variety.

Buying Guide
If you cannot find the soup
pasta, most supermarkets
stock very small macaroni which can
be used as a substitute.

Index